LIFELINES

Help For The Man Drowning In Grief

by Michael Peck

ISBN 978-1-936285-08-2

© Baptist Church Planters 2019

Published by Baptist Church Planters
36830 Royalton Road
Grafton, OH 44044

Web Site: www.bcpusa.org.
Email: bcp@bcpusa.org

Acknowledgements

First and foremost, I want to thank the Lord for His gracious comfort and help on my journey. Let me explain. I came to love the lady who was the little girl I met in the third grade. I was married to her all of my adult life. Then Karen was diagnosed with a very aggressive Stage IV cancer and died after a two-year battle. The grief, sorrow, and adjustments to living without her, even with the support of family and friends, would have been next to impossible without the Lord. I am so indebted to Him, and I want you to know I am so in love with Him! Thank you first and foremost to the Lord for His patience, His lovingkindness, and His strength.

Thank you to President Steve Little and the administration at Baptist Church Planters for their vision in seeing the need for a book such as this. There are many wonderful books for widows, but not too much is available for the man who is in the terrible throes of those first months following the death of his wife. President Little sensed the need for this book and has been an encouragement to me in the writing of it. Thank you, President Little.

A great big thank you to Mrs. Ginny Sebok, the executive administrative assistant of Baptist Church Planters and my editor. Ginny's outstanding editing and her meticulous work as she has poured over the manuscript multiple times is so appreciated. Thank you so much, Ginny.

Thank you to Beth Stevenson who also proofread this manuscript and made suggestions through the rough draft production. Thank you, Beth, for your encouragement.

I certainly want to thank my friends, Don Follet and Eric Wilmeth, for their willingness to share their personal stories of experiencing the Homegoing of their wives, Linda and Amy. I am sure that it was not easy for them to write about their personal experience. It is so helpful and hopeful to read how the Lord worked in their lives. Thank you, Don and Eric.

Thank you to Mellanie Strong for the beautiful cover design and formatting work for the book. It has been such a pleasure working with her over the years. Thank you, Mellanie.

Thank you to my many friends and supporters who not only have prayed for me in writing this manuscript but have even contributed personally toward the production costs that Baptist Church Planters is undertaking. Thank you, dear partners in ministry. It is my desire and wish that the proceeds from the sale of this book go back to Baptist Church Planters. Your investment not only is producing a ministry resource for widowers, you are investing in the great work of missions throughout the United States. Thank you, partners.

Last, but most certainly not least, thank you to my children and grandchildren who love me and have been with me through the cancer journey and are still to this day. I am a greatly blessed man. Thank you, family.

Foreword

You probably don't like the title "widower." I don't, either.

You probably don't feel much like reading. I didn't, either.

You probably don't know how you are going to get through today.
I didn't, either.

In spite of all this, please come on the journey with me. Take your time. You don't have to hurry. But please, continue to read "Lifelines" either from cover to cover or in the separate parts to which you are drawn.

In the months following the Homegoing of my dear Karen, I was crushed and brokenhearted. These are the very "lifelines" I learned from God's Word during those months. They literally were a lifesaver to me. I wish I had had a Lifeline book given to me during those months that was written by someone who loves the Lord, believes the Bible, and had traveled the road ahead of me. You have these in this book.

Please take hold of these Lifelines. Don't try to navigate this by yourself. With the Lord's help, grab His lifelines from His Word. You'll be glad that you did.

Table of Contents

Acknowledgements   iii

Forward   iv

SECTION ONE 1
Getting Acquainted
We probably have a lot in common with each other!

SECTION TWO 4
Reach Out To the Lord Jesus
You need Him more now than *ever* before!

SECTION THREE 11
Step Into the Counseling Center
Four wonderful "doctors" will speak with you!
Paul, Isaiah, Nahum and David

SECTION FOUR 19
The Stories of a Couple of Men
Here's how the Lord can help you as well

SECTION FIVE 34
**Forty Lifelines that Rescue Men Who Feel
Like They Are Drowning in Grief**

SECTION SIX 99
**Fifteen Personal Questions that Widowers Often
Have But are Afraid or Embarrassed to Ask**

SECTION SEVEN 118
This is How I Am Feeling Right Now!
Where in the Bible can I find that lifeline to help me?

SECTION EIGHT 121
**It's Time to Settle the Biggest Decision
You'll Ever Make**
Are you on your way to Heaven?

SECTION ONE

Getting Acquainted
We probably have a lot in common with each other!

We both have experienced
the death of our beloved wives.
We both have wondered
if we are going to survive this!

We can, and we will,
as we turn to the Lord,
allow others to help us,
and apply these Biblical principles.

*You'll never hear me say,
"I know just how you feel."
However! You and I are traveling
on a very similar journey.*

Come with me. Let's get to better know and love the Lord
Jesus.

Please let me introduce myself and say a word about this book.

My name is Michael Peck.

You are holding a book that is written *by* a man *to* men who share a common situation. You and I both have experienced the death of our wives. It sometimes is still hard to believe that she died, isn't it? Yet at other times the reality hits us so hard that we wonder if we are going to survive.

When my Karen died, I was given several books to read by people who loved me and cared about me. These books were big. They were theological. They were heavy. I didn't read them because I simply couldn't. I didn't have the emotional or physical energy.

Does that sound ungrateful?

"I needed the Lord's help. I really did. He is absolutely the lifeline to grab hold of."

I was and still am deeply grateful for their love and concern for me. It's just that in my deepest moments of grief, I didn't have the will or energy to read them. I didn't need hundreds of pages of explanation.

I just needed to know how I was supposed to get through the current day without my wife. How was I ever going to survive without her?

At the time of this writing, it has been nearly three years since Karen died, and obviously I am still here and have survived. Don't misunderstand. I think of her dozens of times a day and miss her more than words can describe. But I have learned how to survive on days that I didn't think I could. Often I just needed a promise or a brief encouragement. I needed to know that what I was feeling was not unique to me. I desperately needed help. I needed the Lord's help, and He is absolutely the lifeline to grab hold of.

I'm eager to share with you, in very brief chapters, how the Lord has helped me and how He wants to help you. When I felt like I was drowning in grief, these biblical principles were lifelines to me.

I want you to grab hold of them as well. You are not alone on the journey. There are many men, just like you, who dearly miss their wives but who are learning to reach out, believe what God says, and grab hold of His lifeline.

You can pick this up and read wherever you wish, or you can start from the beginning and read through to the end.

I'm praying for you!

SECTION TWO

Reach Out to the Lord Jesus

You need Him more now than *ever* before!

You may have been able to
"tough" out lots of situations.
Facing the death of his wife,
a Marine told me, "I've faced
the enemy face to face,
and I survived.
But I don't know if I can survive this."

You don't need to face this alone.
You must not face this alone.

Get to really, really know the Lord Jesus.

Get to know the Lord Jesus in a closer and better way.

The Lord Jesus personally wants to help and comfort you. But it begins by first being sure that you know Him as your personal Savior. If you just know *about* the Lord Jesus without knowing Him *personally*, you will totally miss the wonderful blessing of experiencing the forgiveness of your sins and the amazing security of His redemption. This is not a religion where you try to be good enough to please the Lord. That will never work. It is a relationship with Him because His sacrifice was so good. In the very last section of this book, I share the complete plan God has given to us so that we can truly know Him. If you are not sure about this, STOP! Stop right now, and please go to Section Eight. Place your trust in Him.

Though I've known the Lord as my Savior for many, many years, when my wife died, I was so shattered and brokenhearted that I didn't have very much emotional energy. I knew that I had to be intentional about my walk with the Lord. I had to be intentional in maintaining a good spiritual diet. I had to keep in the Word of God. I may not have had energy to read large portions, but I determined to be intentional about several things.

Knowing Christ. I had to be intentional in my desire to know Christ in a better and deeper way. Paul declared, "That I may know Him and the power of His resurrection, and the fellowship of His sufferings, being conformed to His death" (Philippians 3:10).

Think about what Paul meant. He was intentional as he declared his desire to know Christ. Paul already knew Him as Savior. Now he wanted to really get to know Him better. He wanted to learn more about what Christ's relationship with him was, what His purpose for him was, and the closeness that he could have with the Lord.

In this intense time of sorrow, when waves of grief seem to crash over you, it will be important for you to cry out to the Lord and tell Him that you want to know Him in a far deeper and more personal way.

Picturing My Shepherd. When you trusted Christ to be your Savior, a wonderful eternal relationship began. What peace and help come from knowing that the same Christ Who took your place on the cross and rose again victoriously is the same One Who dearly loves you today! The New Testament has several descriptive pictures of the relationship of Christ and the believer. No picture is any more tender than that of the Shepherd and His sheep.

He said, "I am the good shepherd; and I know My sheep, and am known by My own. My sheep hear My voice, and I know them, and they follow Me" (John 10:14, 27). Throughout these very intense days of sorrow, picture yourself as one of the Lord's sheep and Him as your good shepherd. He knows you. He understands your feelings. He wants to care for you in loving and tender ways. You need to hear His voice. This comes by being in His Word.

I found that reading the Psalms were very good for me. The Psalmist was very honest in describing his severe troubles, but he also was very clear in describing how the Lord answered his cries for help. In the Psalms we see the deepest of sorrows and how David cried out to the Lord. We also see the majesty and the greatness of our God and what He can do.

Discover again the joy of being cherished by Him. Think of what the Lord Jesus said to the Father about you! "Sanctify them by Your truth: Your word is truth" (John 17:17).

The night before the Lord Jesus went to the cross, He prayed in the Garden of Gethsemane. His prayer is intense and intimate. It is frankly stunning to know that we were in His heart as He poured out His heart to the Father. The disciples were the immediate ones in His prayer, but He didn't stop there. He prayed for us! Listen to this, "I do not pray for these alone, but also for those who will believe in Me through their word" (John 17:20). What a glorious position we have. We are sanctified or set apart as something precious for the special use and closeness of the Savior. The more that we are in the Word, the more we will

"It is amazing to realize that the Lord Jesus cherishes you. You may not feel like it, but you really are special to Him."

love Him. That's how it works. No shortcuts. It's through us getting into the Word and the Word getting into us.

You don't have a lot of extra emotional energy right now. In time, this will slowly rebuild and you will grow stronger. But for now, understand that it is normal to have feelings of lifelessness, weakness, emptiness and sometimes exhaustion after doing very little. So you will need to be wise in how you invest your energy.

Determine to be intentional in setting out to know Christ better. Get into His Word. I personally found it so very helpful to read in the Book of the Psalms. The psalmists were so very honest and transparent in describing their trouble. They cried to the Lord, and God answered their cries for help. We see the deepest of sorrows and the majesty of the greatness of our God in the Psalms. Spend some time soon in the Psalms.

He walks on water and will get you back into the boat. What an amazing time of ministry for the disciples and the Lord Jesus. Five thousand men, besides women and children, were served the meal from five small loaves of bread and two fish. You can read about this miracle in Matthew 14:13-21.

The Bible is profound in the simplicity of the description. "He blessed and broke and gave the loaves to the disciples; and the disciples gave to the multitudes. So they all ate and were filled, and they took up twelve baskets full of the fragments that remained" (Matthew 14:19-20).

The disciples must have been worn out. That's a lot of people to serve. I'm sure they were astounded by the ongoing miracle as the bread and fish were immediately multiplied and multiplied. On went the serving of people. Imagine the questions that must have been asked and the many things said to the serving disciples by the amazed recipients of the miraculous meal.

After all this, the disciples were instructed to get back into the boat and cross over the Sea of Galilee. As the boat was piloted by the experienced fishermen on board, heading westerly across the Sea, the Lord Jesus dismissed the multitudes. What a picture-perfect ending to a miraculous day! Right? Not quite!

Somewhere between 3:00 and 6:00 in the morning, the disciples were in trouble. "But the boat was now in the middle of the sea, tossed by the waves, for the wind was contrary" (Matthew 14:24). Think of it. The disciples were in the middle of the Sea, in the middle of the night, in the middle of the storm.

The Lord Jesus came walking to them on the water and, frankly, scared them half to death. When Peter discovered it was the Lord, with an ever-abundance of exuberance, he called out, "Lord, if it is You, command me to come to You on the water" (14:28). The Lord Jesus said, "Come" (14:29).

I have to hand it to Peter. He left the boat. To do so would require him stepping down onto the water and letting go. Say what we want, the other disciples sat in the boat. Peter walked to meet Jesus, and everything was going miraculously well until a sudden gust of wind produced a significant wave, and Peter looked down.

"But when he saw that the wind was boisterous, he was afraid; and beginning to sink he cried out, saying, 'Lord, save me!'" (Matthew 14:30).

How many times a day and night do you find yourself feeling just like Peter must have felt? In the middle of the sea, in the middle of the night, and in the middle of the storm, and there you are, sinking! Rest assured these feelings are normal.

But don't allow yourself to continue sinking. Every time this happens, call out again to the Lord Jesus. He stands, miraculously, waiting to catch you, and think of what He did for Peter. "And immediately Jesus stretched out His hand and caught him, and said to him, 'O you of little faith, why did you doubt?' And when they got into the boat, the wind ceased. Then those who were in the boat came and worshiped Him, saying, 'Truly You are the Son of God'" (Matthew 14:31-33).

The Lord Jesus was close enough to easily catch Peter and safely escort him back to the boat. Even though the winds continued on their walk, they would not last forever. When the two arrived and climbed into the boat, the winds ceased.

Imagine the joy as the disciples exclaimed the sureness of their faith, "You are the Son of God!" Overwhelmed with joy, they continued on their crossing of the Sea.

When my wife Karen died, I was crushed. I mean really crushed. I had very little energy, and even the thought of facing tomorrow without her being with me was totally overwhelming.

I had served the Lord Jesus for forty-seven years as a pastor and missionary administrator. I'd helped dozens of people through times of profound sorrow. I loved the Lord Jesus. I knew all the right answers. I didn't doubt His goodness. But I was out of emotional fuel. I was on empty.

It was not until a few days after the many casseroles were gone and people had returned to their regular living that all alone in my living room, sitting on the spot where Karen would sit, I found myself sinking. "I can't do this, Lord. Help me! Please!" I whispered out loud.

Was I instantly happy? No. Did the sorrow immediately go away? Not by any means. But He gave me the calm, settled assurance that the same sure and solid Hand that had caught Peter would catch me.

"And I give unto them eternal life, and they shall never perish; neither shall anyone snatch them out of My hand. My Father, Who has given them to Me, is greater than all; and no one is able snatch them out of My Father's hand" (John 10:28-29). Both the Father and the Son hold the believer securely in their hands.

I determined that even though I had walked with the Lord for many years, I wanted to know Him better. I wanted my relationship to be deeper.

I had to get into the Word.

I had to talk often with Him and tell Him everything, even if my prayers were brief.

I had to picture His hand that grabbed Peter holding me.

I had to picture Him walking me through this storm and bringing me into the boat.

I had to picture that the winds would eventually slowly start to calm down. For the disciples, the winds calmed immediately. For us, the winds will slowly calm down.

Grab hold of this. We are in the most intense time of our sorrow. But don't let wasted time go by. While you don't have a lot of strength, you can determine to really get to know the Lord Jesus far better and much deeper.

SECTION THREE

Step Into the Counseling Center

Doctors Paul, Isaiah, Nahum and David
Will Speak with You Now!

I've selected four men
from Scripture who have been
greatly used of the Lord
in my personal life.
God's Word written by them
will greatly bless you as well.

"Dr. Paul" says, "Let me be straight up but gentle with you!"

You know what it means to be straight up with someone, right? It means to be honest, to be totally open, and not to mix the truth with anything that is untrue.

I want to be totally honest with you and yet gentle at the same time. The Apostle Paul was a rugged man. He endured beatings, stoning, and shipwrecks, and yet he courageously pushed on. He was an incredible man of strength and determination. But he was more than that. He also knew how to be loving, caring, and gentle.

"Embrace the truth. Don't run from it. Face it with the Lord's help."

Paul's straight up but gentleness. That's what he wrote to the folks at Ephesus. Listen to this. "But, speaking the truth in love…" (Ephesians 4:15). Truth without love is harsh and brutal. Love without truth is not love at all. It is deception and the withholding of helpfulness. Throughout this little book, I will be straight up and very honest with you. But I will try to be tender and gentle as well.

Straight up

- You have experienced the death of your wife and these, for sure, are going to be the hardest days of your life.
- You may be surprised by the depths of the emotional pain that you are feeling right now. You didn't know it could hurt so badly.
- You cannot imagine living without her.
- You feel bewildered, empty, confused and crushed. It may sound strange to say, but frankly, your heart is broken. Maybe it would be better to say that your heart is shattered.
- You may even be experiencing times of anger and resentment toward the Lord. "Why did my wife have to die?" is the question that tears at your heart.

Gentle

You are not alone. There are many of us on this trail with you. Let me speak the truth in love to you. You have handled many things in life. However! You cannot handle this alone. If you know Christ as your Savior, you won't travel this alone. He wants to hold you closely and help you through this day. If you aren't sure about your relationship with Him, please go to www.michaelpeck.org and click "Heaven! Are You Going There?"

Paul has some great news for you to embrace. He shares truth in a loving way, acknowledging that hard times are not easy but that there is something special for us to really embrace. Think of several of these tremendous principles from "Dr. Paul."

Keep eternity in view. Never are we to live in denial and pretend that all is well when it isn't. There is nothing manly nor is there anything spiritual about pretending to be a tower of courage when your heart is breaking and you feel like you're not even sure how to navigate another day.

Paul has some very good words of advice about our view. Listen to what he wrote. "Therefore we do not lose heart. Even though our outward man is perishing, yet the inward man is being renewed day by day. For our light affliction, which is but for a moment, is working for us a far more exceeding and eternal weight of glory" (2 Corinthians 4:16-17).

On one hand, view your problems, sorrow, and heartache. Now on the other hand, try to imagine the glory of eternity. Forever, and ever, and ever, and ever we will be with the Lord and our redeemed loved ones. Forever and ever! Glory!

Thanks, "Dr. Paul." You have spoken the truth in love. Our bodies are wearing out. Our affliction is real. But in comparison with eternity, our affliction is "light" and brief.

Think about that.

A e | 14

"Dr. Isaiah" says, "Remember this when you are feeling so weak."

Perhaps you have been surprised how exhausting grief can be. So many painful thoughts are flooding over you. Believe it or not, this is very normal. You are not losing your mind.

"Grief is huge. It affects every area of our being."

I remember the many times that people described their feelings of grief. Sorrow, sadness, loneliness, and confusion were often described. I too have experienced all of these. But there is something else that almost always was part of the description. I can hear the many voices saying, "And I am exhausted. I just don't have the energy to do anything. Why am I always so tired?"

It's because grief is huge. It affects every area of our being. At times we just can't eat and, in fact, go quite a while without a nourishing meal. The opposite can be true as well. Many resort to eating, way overeating, as a means of comfort. Many have told of the bag of chips, fast food, constant munching especially in the evenings. It is a lonely time. You have been used to having the companionship of your wife, and now part of your life is missing.

Sometimes it is just so difficult to sleep. You know that it is important to sleep, but it just won't come. Your bed always had two in it. Now the other side of the bed is empty, and nightly as you slip into your side, her absence is unbearable, and sleep eludes you. If your sleeplessness is becoming a pattern, you really must speak with your Primary Care Physician. I know you don't want to, but you know that you must.

With all these things and with the enormous energy being used to mourn and grieve, don't be surprised if you feel the weakest you've ever felt. Isaiah wants to have a word with you about this very important subject.

Isaiah's promise for when we are the weakest. With the Lord's help, you WILL get through this one day at a time. "Fear not, for I am with you; Be not dismayed, for I am your God. I will strengthen you, Yes, I will help you, I will uphold you with My righteous right hand" (Isaiah 41:10).

Thanks, "Dr. Isaiah." It is amazing how terribly weak and fearful we can become. It is tremendous as we consider the amazing way that the Lord reaches into our lives and reassures us that because He is our God, we do not have to fear. We do not have remain in a state of being dismayed. He will help us and strengthen us, and He will hold us. We need to be reminded often of this wonderful promise.

Think about that!

"Dr. Nahum" says, "The goodness of God even in our trouble!"

It may have been a little while since you have read the Old Testament book of Nahum. Nineveh was the capital of the extremely cruel and wicked Assyrian Empire. One-and-a-half centuries before this, God had sent another prophet, Jonah, to that wicked capital city. As you know, they believed God's message, and a widespread revival broke out.

Apparently they either didn't tell their children and grandchildren or their descendants didn't believe them. Now Nahum is commissioned to preach that sure judgment is coming.

Make no mistake about it, Nahum pointedly tells them that God is majestic and powerful. His judgment and wrath are about to break out upon them. In a very dramatic way, God describes His judgment in all His fury.

Sandwiched into this fiery message of judgment shines a bright and beautiful verse that is important for us today. While I don't know the road you have traveled before the Homegoing of your wife, I know that "trouble" is probably a word that you would use to describe your road right now.

Everything is so different. Emotions are raw. Tears are frequent. Lonely times are horrible. "Dr. Nahum" has a word for us. Listen to what he says.

"The LORD is good, A stronghold in the day of trouble; And He knows those who trust in Him" (Nahum 1:7).

The Person. "The LORD is good." The idea of this goodness of the LORD is His kindness and beauty. I know that there are those who might very well be wondering, "If the LORD is so good, why did my wife die?"

I don't want to sound like there are simple, little answers to such a profound question. But honestly, as we go back to Genesis, everything changed when sin came into the world. God warned Adam, "But of the tree of the knowledge of good and evil you shall not eat, for in the day that you eat of it you shall surely die" (Genesis 2:17). You know that in the very next chapter, they ate, sin entered, spiritual death took place, and the process of physical death started.

We all experience the heartache of death because of the entrance of sin. But in spite of the heartache, I can tell you for sure that God remains good. If you will look to Him and give Him time, you will spot His beauty and His kindness. You really will.

The Protection. "A stronghold in the day of trouble." The "stronghold" speaks of a place of safety, a place of safe refuge from the trouble that is swirling around us. We have no guarantee that we will be kept from trouble. But in the trouble, those who know Christ in a personal, saving way will discover His wonderful refuge and strength.

You must not think that you are strong enough to go it alone.

You must not think that you are wise enough to figure everything out by yourself.

You need Him, and He longs to be your stronghold. It is an amazing thing to discover that when you are in the stronghold, when you are close to Him, even though your heart is broken, you will see the beauty, the kindness, the goodness of the Lord.

The Promise. "And He knows those who trust in Him."

I have a hard time fathoming this. I believe it. I rejoice in it. It is just hard for me to wrap my head around the fact that the Lord knows me. Not just casually acquainted is the Lord with His people. The word "knows" is *yada* (ya-DAH). Are you ready for this? The idea of this word is "to perceive, to know by experience, to know in an intimate way."

> *"I am awed at this. How can someone like me be in the intimate, personal, intentional knowledge of One so high and awesome?"*

I am hushed at this. How can someone like me be in the intimate, personal, intentional knowledge of One so high and awesome? I am not sure I will ever fully understand this. However, I can rejoice in it.

Thanks, "Dr. Nahum," for reminding us that even in these days, weeks, and months of terrible trouble and heartache, we need to be watching for Him. Run to Him as your stronghold. The closer you draw to Him, the more you will see His hand of goodness. He knows you and wants to help you trust Him more and more. Isn't it strange how these two words are in the same verse, even the same breath? "Goodness" and "trouble." They meet by being in His "stronghold."

Think about that!

"Dr. David" says, "Feeling overwhelmed? I've just the thing for you."

I've saved the last appointment with "Dr. David," the King of Israel. Listen to what he says to us in Psalm 142:3, "When my spirit was overwhelmed within me, Then You knew my path."

The idea of being "overwhelmed" has to do with "feeling like things are crashing over us like mighty waves of the ocean." The actual word is *ataph* (a-TAF). The literal meaning is "to cover over, to be faint."

During Karen's lengthy illness and subsequent Homegoing, there were plenty of times that I felt overwhelmed. I still do and probably will still have these feelings in the future.

David felt overwhelmed. Do you have the little tiny words in your Bible in between the Psalm number and the first verse? These are called "superscriptions." They describe the setting of the Psalm. The superscription for Psalm 142 states that the setting of this Psalm was when David was in the cave.

David's situation. So we discover that David is in a cave. That might not sound so bad, except that there are two different possible settings for this to take place. The first could be in 1 Samuel 22 at the cave of Adullam where we read, "David therefore departed from there and escaped to the cave of Adullam. So when his brothers and all of his father's house heard it, they went down there to him. And everyone who was in distress, everyone who was in debt, and everyone who was discontented gathered to him. So he became captain over them. And there were about four hundred men with him" (1 Samuel 22:1-2). That sounds "overwhelming" to me.

The other cave experience was at En Gedi as found in 1 Samuel 24:1-2, "Take note! David is in the Wilderness of En Gedi. Then Saul took three thousand chosen men from all Israel, and went to seek David and his men." That also sounds "overwhelming" to me.

Either cave experience is horrible and overwhelming from a human perspective.

David's satisfaction. There was something so calming, so reassuring to David, and that was remembering that the Lord knew his path. This actually means that the Lord knew the direction of David's life, the way he should go, and the plans that the Lord would be working throughout David's circumstances.

Thanks, "Dr. David," for reminding us that in the overwhelming moments, the Lord knows right where we are, just what we need, and which way we should be going as we walk with Him. He knows our path. He understands our journey. He knows.

Think about that.

SECTION FOUR

The Stories of a Couple of Men

We don't have all the answers.
However!
We have traveled the path
on which you are traveling right now.

Here are the stories
of how the Lord
is helping us
and how He will help you.

Let me share "My Story" with you.

It is my story of how my children and grandchildren walked with us on a very long and difficult road battling cancer.

I call her "My Karen."

It actually was the third grade when we first met, and yes, we grew up together. By the middle of our senior year in high school, I managed to finally work up the courage to ask her out on a date. She said, "Yes," and we never dated anyone else.

We were married on December 11th, 1971. She completed her two years at Bible college, and I was in the middle of my junior year studying for the ministry. We were only twenty, and hardly had two nickels to rub together. But with her parents' permission and the blessing from mine, we were joyfully married and began our lives together as husband and wife.

Our forty-five years of marriage flew by quickly. We loved being pastor and wife in several churches as well as being missionaries with Baptist Church Planters. I served as the vice president, and she served as the director of JOY Club ministries to children.

Though far from perfect, I mean, very far from perfect, we loved being married to each other. Through birth and adoption the Lord gave us ten precious children and very special grandchildren.

Then February 24th, 2015, seemingly came out of nowhere. With no symptoms other than a slight cough for a couple of days, Karen was diagnosed with Stage 4 lung cancer.

How could this beautiful and very healthy lady have cancer? She never smoked and was never around secondhand smoke. I was blindsided. On April 4th, 2017, as I held her, my precious Karen went Home to be with the Lord.

I didn't think I could go on.

I didn't even want to go on without her. No, I was not suicidal. I was crushed. I needed to cry out to the Lord for help.

Does this sound similar to where you are right now? The Lord wants to help both you and me through these deep waters. In our distress, we need to call upon the Lord.

I couldn't face this on my own. I needed the Lord. He really helped me and will help you as well, if you will let Him. "In my distress I called upon the LORD, And cried out to my God; He heard my voice from His temple, And my cry came before Him, even to His ears" (Psalm 18:6).

Her cancer came as a sudden, unexpected shock. She was in such perfect health. She never smoked and never was around secondhand smoke. When she developed a slight cough, we assumed that she was getting bronchitis and perhaps needed an antibiotic. All of us, including her medical team, were stunned to discover that she had Stage IV lung cancer.

Karen never lived in denial about her cancer, even though she didn't feel sick at first.

The second day of her hospitalization, as the family and friends left her hospital room, we had some alone time together. I sat at her bedside holding her hand. It was with all my strength I tried fighting back my tears. Looking at her, I saw the most beautiful lady in the entire world with a very special peace (not denial), a genuine quietness and confidence.

She quietly said, "Honey. The tests are going to come back cancerous. As I was praying about it in the night, I just had this settled certainty come into my heart. It's going to be cancer, and it is going to be very serious. I told the Lord that I was not going to waste energy asking 'why?' I was going to use all the strength that the Lord would give me to live by the 'what?' I want to ask the Lord 'what do You want me to do and how can I glorify You?' Michael, I am glad that you are going on the journey with me, Honey. I am just so sorry for you."

Sorry for me? At that point the tears came by the bucketsful. I was just so sorry for her.

She was right. It was cancer, and it was indeed serious.

It would be several years later that I discovered what she wrote in the front cover of her Bible. This is what she wrote: "February 24th, 2015. Stage IV Lung Cancer. Not 'Why" but rather, 'What' do You want me to do? May Christ be glorified in my life."

I have come back often to her little writing. Don't ask *why*. Be sure to ask *what*. The more I ask "why" the worse my condition is. How much wiser and better it is to ask "what" do You, Lord, want me to do, and how can I bring glory to You throughout this?

"Whatever you do, do all to the glory of God" (1 Corinthians 10:31). The more you ask *why,* the worse it will be. Start asking the Lord *what* do You want me to learn about You and what do You want me to do?

A little over two years later, after traveling down a very difficult road of trying to treat the cancer, Karen went Home to be with the Lord. The obituary in the newspaper read, "Karen is survived by her husband Michael and her children...."

But I surely didn't feel like a survivor. Probably that is just exactly how you feel as well.

The word picture was so vivid to me that night at 10:36 on April 4th. You see, the Christian life is like a race that is being run. Any race has a starting point, a finish line, and a whole lot of course to be covered in between. Nearing his own death, Paul wrote, "I have fought the good fight, I have finished the race, I have kept the faith" (2 Timothy 4:7).

Karen ran her race. She ran it very well. Throughout her cancer journey, she was faithful in keeping her focus on Christ. She was always more concerned about me as well as her children and grandchildren than she was about herself. That was how my Karen lived her life. She was often more concerned about others than for herself.

My grown children wanted and needed to know the truth, the whole truth, and nothing but the truth. They walked with us. They helped their own children face the hard fact that Grandma wasn't getting better. Pastors, friends, family, neighbors, and even the medical team, were wonderful. But it was in the middle of the night as I sat by her bedside that I sensed, in the most profound of ways, the emotions of grief, aloneness, and the slow tearing away of part of my life.

"Karen's race was completed. She finished her race. She very quietly died in my arms but soared over her finish line. I was so proud of her and so happy for her. But I was so profoundly broken."

And then a few days later, Karen's race was completed. She finished her race. She very quietly died in my arms but soared over her finish line. I was so proud of her and so happy for her. But I was so profoundly broken.

Crushed. Shattered. Brokenhearted.

It was like ripping a piece of paper in half. The jagged piece remaining was just how I felt. It doesn't sound much like being a survivor, does it? I wanted to sit at her finish line. I didn't want to go on without her. I didn't know if I could go on.

But here I am now three years later. I still miss her every day. But I am surviving because of the Lord's mercy and help. Though I already knew it, I truly am experiencing the love and compassion of the Lord. He wants to wrap you up in His love and compassion, if you will turn to Him. Cry out to Him.

Think of the incredible help that is available to you.

"He heals the brokenhearted and binds up their wounds. He counts the number of the stars; He calls them all by name" (Psalm 147:3-4). Think of it! The Lord knows the exact number of stars, and He has assigned a different name to each of them, and yet He knows you as an individual and wants to heal your broken heart in time, if you will turn to Him.

My Prayer for You and Myself

Long ago the Apostle Paul prayed a very powerful and personal request of the Lord for the folks who were dear to him at Ephesus.

He prayed and asked the Lord to do several wonderful things for them.

First, he prayed that they would come to a deeper knowledge of the Lord. "That the God of our Lord Jesus Christ, the Father of glory, may give to you the spirit of wisdom and revelation in the knowledge of Him" (Ephesians 1:17).

Right now you and I really need to know the Lord Jesus in a deeper way. We need to call out to Him, determine to know Him better, and discover more about Him through His Word and prayer.

Second, he prayed that their understanding would have His light shining upon it. "The eyes of your understanding being enlightened" (Ephesians 1:18a).

He wants us to not waste our energy trying to understand those things that probably we'll never fully understand in this life. The death of our sweethearts was not an accident nor is it a waste. We must not spin our wheels trying to figure out why this has happened. Now we need to trust Him, really trust Him and believe that He has a plan and purpose. Even if we can't understand why He allowed this, we will seek His understanding.

Third, he prayed that they would know the security that they have in Christ. "That you may know what is the hope of His calling, what are the riches of the glory of His inheritance in the saints" (Ephesians 1:18b).

Right now it pretty much feels like our world is shattered into tiny pieces.

At times it is hard to concentrate and terribly difficult to make decisions.

The loneliness is overwhelming, and nothing is the same.

That's why the security that we have in Christ Jesus the Lord is so amazing. He's got us! He will not only get us through, He has big plans for us in the future. We have a settled calling. We have riches in our glorious inheritance. Regardless of how you and I might "feel" at this moment, we are set apart unto Himself. We are secure.

Fourth, he prayed that they would grasp the mighty power of the Lord available to them. "And what is the exceeding greatness of His power toward us who believe, according to the working of His mighty power which He worked in Christ when He raised Him from the dead and seated Him at His right hand in the heavenly places" (Ephesians 1:19-20).

You and I must not face this alone. We just must not…and we don't have to.

The same incredible power that raised Christ from the dead on that Sunday morning long ago is the exact same incredible power that is available to us as well. You and I need the Lord and His power.

Together we need to intentionally direct our energies toward getting to know the Lord Jesus in a deeper way. While not denying our painful grief, when we focus on the Lord Jesus we will discover that He is both extremely glorious and yet very gracious. He really cares about us. Let Him help you. You can't do this alone.

I'm praying for you.

The word "hope" in Ephesians 1:18 is not wishful thinking. It is the confidence and assurance that the Lord gives to His people. Your confidence in the Lord will grow stronger as you invest time with the Lord Jesus in His Word and prayer.

Let Me Share "Don's Story" With You.

It is the story of Don Follet and the sudden, unforeseen Homegoing of his wife, Linda. Don has adult children and grandchildren.

When Linda and I were married, we established a long-term commitment with God as the center of our lives. We were thankful for the two great children He allowed us to raise in a Godly home and church family. God provided some very dear friends to laugh and shed tears with us as we sought to serve the Lord. I am very thankful that today they still stand with me as God directs me on a new path.

Linda and I met at my home in New Milford, PA, at the end of October 1965. She was in the second group of nursing students my sister brought home from Robert Packer School of Nursing. She attracted me when my mother asked me to go to the store for sausage and she volunteered to go and assist in the proper choice. The next weekend I asked her to do a little socializing with me and she agreed. I had the feeling she might be the one God wanted for me, but she was not convinced as yet. We dated most weekends for the next three years, and apparently our relationship grew even when she was on affiliation in Philadelphia, PA. I asked her to marry me on February 3, 1967, in a bowling alley parking lot because I was too excited to wait any longer. She said yes and we were married on September 21, 1968, after she graduated from nursing school. We traveled to Bermuda for our honeymoon and subsequently resided in an apartment in Vestal, NY, before buying a home in Conklin, NY, a year later. Three years later, we started our family and remained very active in the youth and many other ministries of our local church. Linda worked at a hospital and doctor's office before and after our children were raised. She continued in a doctor's office after my work moved us to Texas. We both retired in January 2007 in order to travel and see the beautiful things of the world that God has created. Our retirement trip was a cruise to the Mediterranean which was a cherished but very busy trip. In the next 10 years, we traveled extensively while taking time to vacation with friends and family and remain very active in our local church. What a blessing God provided!

Now for some thoughts about how one day God changed my perspective in a short period of time in June of 2017. Linda had not felt well over the weekend and on Monday morning we went to the doctor. He provided a prescription and indicated it should provide relief. She took the medicine but late in the day, she found it very difficult to swallow and further had a great deal of difficulty breathing. I decided it was time for the emergency room and she concurred. We talked on the way to the hospital but the verbal communication was limited after that.

By the time she was placed in a room, she was no longer conversant. They ran all sorts of tests but the results provided no insight to her difficulties. The surgeon indicated he would have to do exploratory surgery to determine the cause of her difficulty. My daughter and I felt her squeeze our hands as she went off to surgery. We thought she might have gotten a glimpse of heaven and was telling us she may not return from surgery. Thankfully, following Linda's example, we were able to let the staff and doctors know that Linda knew the Lord as her Savior and would be going to heaven if that was now the Lord's plan. The surgeon later came out to tell me that she had experienced a blood clot that had affected several organs but that she was not stable enough to do more exploratory surgery at the moment. Back in the room, I learned that the clot had done so much damage that she would not likely live through the night and that I would have to make a decision whether they should do everything possible to keep her alive. I ultimately decided with much difficulty and tears that they should just keep her comfortable since the damage was not recoverable. This was a very hard moment and I prayed for the Lord's strength since the decision had occurred so abruptly. My feeling at that point was a desire to talk with her one last time but based on medical advice, I decided not to keep her from being promoted to heaven.

Linda and I had known each other in excess of 50 years and the Lord enabled us to have a great life together through almost 49 years of marriage. Over the last several years, Linda had experienced a great deal of pain which resulted in multiple spinal surgeries. She was always a real testimony to the staff during hospital stays. I prayed earnestly that God would take away her pain and that is exactly what He did according to His perfect plan, not certainly in the way I was thinking He would relieve her pain. Our love for each other kept us together and that love has never wavered even now. Surely, this very specific prayer request was answered in God's time. Linda was my strength and encouragement and provided wise guidance when I needed it without fail. I struggle because we did everything together and now, I trust the Lord to show me how to accomplish things without her. My experience so far is that the road is very difficult, but I thank the Lord for His daily guidance (more like minute by minute). Thank the Lord as well for His promise of Ps 46:1 where it says "God is our refuge and strength, A very present help in trouble." I could not make it without God and His sufficient grace.

"I am learning that God is always with me, and certainly One who can walk on the water among other miracles can keep me on the right path."

What am I thinking and feeling during this difficult time in my life? I am sensing a tremendous loss, and recovery seems a long way off, even after more than two years. I am feeling like part of me is gone as well, sort of like I lost a limb. God chose to take Linda home over what I thought was a very short period of time when I least expected it and thereby relieved her of any further pain for which I am extremely thankful. I sometimes wander about the house now feeling that a big part of my life is missing and wonder what task to start next. That is when I go to the Word and let the Lord give me the strength I need as He promised. I am still very much in love with Linda and miss her more than can be measured at this point. I often wondered if I was always doing enough for her but when asked, she would always tell me that I took care of all her needs and more too. My memories of her last hours on earth make me wonder about that even though many have told me I did all I could have done. For a long time after Linda's heavenly promotion, I wanted to talk about it but could not do so without tears. Today, I want to talk about the blessing Linda was to me even though there still may be tears. God sent the right woman to me (Prov 31:12) and for that I am very thankful.

I am learning that God is always with me, and certainly One who can walk on the water among other miracles can keep me on the right path if I keep my eyes on Him and keep hold of His extended hand which gives me the peace He promised. I am reminded of Isaiah 26:3 which says, "You will keep him in perfect peace, Whose mind is stayed on You, Because he trusts in You." He knows what is best and we do not. This definitely is a growing experience but I know that just as Job could not stand in judgment of why God does things, neither can I. I find that I have to go back to the Word when I am struggling and be still and listen to God give me insight. I am attempting to move on but the steps are still very small. I keep asking the Lord for wisdom and discernment to not replace God's insight through the Word but to replace Linda's valuable input from a human sense. Something as simple as going to church without her causes me to struggle not because of the message or the people but for the fact that she was always there when possible sitting next to me. I now sit alone with Linda's seat vacant. Sometimes the thoughts overwhelm me and I find the need to leave quickly. God is giving me strength as I need it. Thankfully, God knows what we need. God for sure is an ever-present help in time of need. God is training me and leading me down a path to eternity and I find myself looking up awaiting His return. Praise the Lord! His promises are truly a blessing. He has given me a ministry to work with others who have lost spouses. I can understand their situation and share how God is helping me. Others who have not experienced the loss of a spouse may not be able to relate. There will be tears that others may not understand but God does give us precious memories that bring joy even though our hearts may still be broken. God does promise to heal the broken heart but His timing is not the same as ours.

I find it difficult to be involved with things Linda and I used to do as a couple. Thank the Lord, my family has been very helpful from that perspective. Actually, what keeps me going are the memories of what the Lord allowed us to do and the joys we had doing them while always holding each other's hand. Those hands passed non-verbal communication. What a blessed hope we have that we will see our loved ones again. God chose to send Linda to me for the training I needed and it appears that He felt the training was sufficient and that she could go to her real home. With God's help and the assistance of family and friends, I am using Linda's valued instruction. Is it easy? The answer is no. As the song goes…it is not an easy road but the good news is that the path leads to heaven. In God's time, I am going to heaven and though I have to wait, I have a responsibility to win the lost and help others with circumstances like mine.

There is a song that has had special meaning during this period of my Christian growth. The lyrics were written by Dora Greenwell (1821-1882), and the first verse goes as follows:

I am not skilled to understand

> What God hath willed, what God hath planned;
> I only know at His right hand
> Stands one who is my Savior.

It is not important that we understand. It is only important that we trust God. He has promised a place prepared for us and I look forward to eternity with Him according to His timing.

I rejoice in the fact that Linda is home even though I am saddened at the moment because of my great love for her, I look forward to seeing her again soon. Soon our tears will be wiped away (Rev 21:4) and we will spend our time honoring Christ. Linda just got a head start. This world is not my home. We are sojourners just passing through while being trained.

Let Me Share "Eric's Story" With You.

It is the story of Eric Wilmeth and the dynamics of the Homegoing of his wife Amy. Eric has children at home who have walked through this with him.

God is faithful! He has been since before the foundations of time, to this very moment, through the end of eternity.

> "The steadfast love of the LORD never ceases;
> his mercies never come to an end;
> they are new every morning;
> great is your faithfulness"
> Lamentations 3:22-23 (ESV).

As I write this it has been three years since I got to spend the final 24 hours with Amy before her faith was made sight and she got the glorious experience of seeing God face to face. We had 18 years 4 months and 23 days together as husband and wife. We were high school sweethearts and best friends. We never wanted to be apart. When asked what my greatest fear was, I always answered losing Amy. I hated stories where the wife had passed away in childbirth, and I was a bit fearful when she became pregnant with our first child. Faith was born in 2003; she and her mom were both healthy as could be. Each additional child brought more worry but for no reason as Adam was born healthy as was his mom in '06 and Ethan in '08. In fact, if it hadn't been for pregnancy, I'm not sure if Amy would have ever had to go to the doctor!

In 2011, though, she found a small lump. I remember the day we got the official word from the doctor that it was cancer. We were back home sorting out the news, in shock and trying to figure out what was next. I began crying, sobbing really, and she comforted me. She said it would be alright, and I cried that I didn't want to lose her. "You won't lose me," she told me gently and calmly. She had cancer, had peace, and comforted me.

Over the next years we had lots of ups and downs. Many doctor visits, surgeries, treatments, and opportunities to be used for God's good. God constantly showed Himself faithful as I fought through my fear and gave my Amy to my God. She was always His anyways, but He graciously gave me time to let go of my fear and grow in my faith as I experienced Him more.

There are so many things God did to display His mercies to me and my family. If you read back through Amy's blogs, you will see many of them (not least of which is our miracle baby, Asher, born in 2013 amidst the cancer fight). Three years ago today though, His mercy extended even further in my life as I spent those last hours by Amy's side. The kids' bedtime had come that evening, so they each told Mom goodnight. I went and prayed with them, then returned to Amy's side along with her parents. Not long after that her body failed, and she entered the arms of Jesus, the Author and Completer of her faith. I cried out to God, worshiping Him in my tears for all His wonderful blessings and goodness. He had healed Amy and lovingly, faithfully wrapped His arms around me.

"I can't imagine what Amy has experienced these last three years being in the presence of God."

A lot of the next days were nothing more than blurs. I know I made a lot of decisions and got things done, but I don't think I could detail them for you.

I was overwhelmed daily by the outpouring of love and support for me and the kids. I was blown away by the number of friends and family that showed up at her celebration of life service and reception. I continued to be in awe of God's faithfulness as cards continued to come and people kept checking in on me those next few months. God faithfully kept me focused on His mercies through the many servants He chose to use.

The cards eventually stopped showing up and the check-ins waned down to the closest of friends as is always the case as life goes on. Yet God is always faithful, always worthy to be praised. The kids and I kept walking forward day by day. The beginning of the grief journey was much like the cancer fight: keep trusting Jesus, leaning on the Holy Spirit, worshiping God, one step at a time, one breath at a time.

I can't imagine what Amy has experienced these last three years being in the presence of God. Thanks to a wonderful gift from my uncle, I was able to study more in depth what Scripture has to say about that topic. God's Word has a way of doing that for us. The truth found in its pages comforts like nothing else can. When we think on what is true, honorable, just, pure, lovely, commendable, excellent, or praiseworthy, and we put it into practice in our lives, then the God of peace is always with us (Philippians 4:8-9). Each day proved to be insurmountably hard for me to navigate until I let God's Word fill me to keep my eyes fixed on Him instead of my circumstances. I knew the best way I could care for the kids was to lean more on Christ. In the months after Amy's death I felt more alone than I thought possible, yet I felt closer to God and more comforted by Him.

I prayed for wisdom for each day. How to father the kids without Amy. How to manage responsibilities of the kids, ministry, home care, and work. I even prayed to not miss God's direction if I was to remain single or not (I honestly didn't want to make the wrong choice in following God's plan for me). God faithfully, daily, answered my prayers as the kids and I stepped forward day by day. God met all our needs and provided wonderfully, but He also made it obviously plain to me that He did not want me raising these four kids on my own. He had given me the skills needed, but my heart lacked all that is required for the task, and I knew God would bring someone into my life to provide exactly what I needed and what the kids would need in the days ahead. I began praying for that future day when God would answer this new prayer, never expecting for Him to answer so quickly!

Jacy was introduced to me in June of 2017, and it didn't take long for her and me to see that God was faithful in providing us for each other. Our relationship status moved quickly to "when" we would get married, not "if."

Amy expected God's continued provision for me and the kids. In a final letter to me she wrote, "Life is but a vapor. Live it to the fullest! Don't miss the opportunities God places in your path!" She faithfully served her faithful God and desired His will above her own. She encouraged me to live life with no regrets, always choosing God's will over my own.

God's constant love, faithfulness, and provision doesn't mean these last three years have been easy. It does not mean I have made all good choices or always responded correctly to my grief or the stresses of life. It does not mean I have not cried and grieved. On the contrary, grief is a fickle and unpredictable thing that grabs ahold at the drop of a hat some days as I miss Amy and remember her. Many days have come with tears, but all the days have contained worship of my Lord and Savior, my Rock, and my Shelter. God has continued to grow my faith and trust in Him, and I know He will continue until the day when I see my Lord face to face as Amy has. Oh, what a day that will be! (But not yet, God isn't done with me yet!)

SECTION FIVE

Forty Lifelines That Rescue Men
Who Feel Like They are Drowning in Grief

These are some of the lifelines that got me through
those terrible first months!

I know they will get you through, too!

*What I am going to share with you
is wonderful for the best of your days
as well as powerful for the worst of your days.*

Feel free to read this section in any order,
depending on the situation you are facing on a given day.
Be sure to give special thought to the Scriptures
and to the "grab hold of this" at the end of each reading.
This is more than some "theory."
Drowning man, I want to tell you, these are the powerful
Biblical truths that got me through when I didn't think I
was going to make it.

These Forty Situations are Exactly Where the Lord Jesus Wants to Meet Us!

Sooner or later you will experience these forty situations. Keep the guide nearby to turn to it quickly. Read these over and over again. These forty lifelines will indeed keep you from sinking.

1 In Your Worst of News There Is Good News

2 John 14 Has a Whole New Meaning, Doesn't It?

3 You're in a Great Storm. Run to Your Refuge

4 Getting Through the Day. Don't Forget This

5 Can't Sleep? Here's Something for the Middle of the Night

6 Promise Me That You Won't Be Bitter Toward the Lord

7 Please, Lord! Either Calm the Storm or Calm Me

8 Men Who Can Fix Anything and Those Who Can't

9 If God Loves Me So Much, Why Did He Say "No"?

10 Oh, Wow! Just What I Need for this Moment

11 Am I Going Crazy? I've Never Felt So Badly

12 Don't You Wish Someone Would Tell Your Friends What Not to Say?

13 The Hurt is Real But So Is the Lord

14 Wonderful Help from a Wonderful Person Waiting for You

15 Give Me Even Just a Little Encouragement Today

16 Can You Believe That Someone Told Me To Keep A Stiff Upper Lip?

17 I'm Out Of Gas and I Can't Go On

18 Getting Through Today. Embrace the Race

19 You Might Not Look Wooly, But You Do Have a Good Shepherd

20 He Counts the Stars and Names Them, But Heals Your Heart, Too

21 His Grace is Sufficient. It Really is Enough

22 What a Profound Difference for Those Who Know Christ

23 He Knows How We Feel. Others Guess. But He Knows

24 The 80/20 Principle You and I Are in Right Now

25 Two Widowers in the Same Pew but Worlds Apart

26 When the Lord Jesus Brings Us to His Father's House

27 Convinced That God Is Just Who He Says He Is

28 Some Say to Follow Your Heart. God Says "Guard It"

29 Are You Having a "Batach" Kind of Day

30 Faith That Pleases the Lord and Gets Me Through Today

31 These Tears Aren't Forever

32 You Might Need to Use Your Middle Name on Yourself

33 Have You Ever Wondered Why Jesus Cried?

34 Settle Down and Be Still. You'll Discover Something Wonderful

35 These Troubles Aren't Forever

36 Be Patient. The Train is Coming!

37 I Just Feel So Much Regret. Is There Help for Me?

38 Won't It Be Grand When Sorrow and Mourning Shall Flee Away?

39 In Your Sorrow, Don't Lost Sight of What's Precious!

40 Everyone is So Happy and I Feel So Alone and Sad

Lifeline # 1
In Your Worst of News There Is Good News

The worst of news might have come in the form of your wife's diagnosis or perhaps the solemn words of the physician, "I am sorry. We did all we could to save her." Whatever the "worst" of news you have heard and faced, there is some good news that will be very important to grab hold of.

Lazarus died. His sisters Mary and Martha deeply grieved and could not imagine living without him. Tenderly the Lord Jesus said to Martha, "I am the resurrection and the life. He who believes in Me, though he may die, he shall live. And whoever lives and believes in Me shall never die. Do you believe this?" (John 11:25-26).

I'm thinking of Phil. He had never known the depths of pain and sorrow that he felt that day. Rain softly fell upon the small assembly of family and very close friends as the preacher spoke at the graveside. Several days before this, his wife had gone Home to be with the Lord, and at the present moment he didn't think that he could possibly go on without her.

The kind pastor explained that the powerful truth of Christ's statement in John 11:25 didn't mean that those who believe in Him would never die physically. The preacher explained that those who believe in the Lord Jesus and trust Him to be their Savior would never die spiritually. They'd never be separated from the Lord.

Phil's sorrow was great, but his assurance was greater. He was assured that his wife knew the Lord and that she was with Him. He still was devasted, but how glad he was that Christ arose.

Christ's resurrection changes everything. Right now in the deepest moments of despair and sorrow, focus on this truth today. Christ conquered death. He rose and is alive. The One to Whom you can pray, trust, depend upon, learn more about, and even walk with by faith today is alive. There is wonderful comfort in this very good news.

Grab hold of this. The Lord Jesus experienced death on the cross for our sins. But the grave could not keep Him. Death could not hold Him. It is wonderful, absolutely wonderful, to remember today that the Lord Jesus says to us, "I am the resurrection and the life" (John 11:25). Incredible help and power are made available to you because He arose.

Lifeline # 2
John 14 Has a Whole New Meaning, Doesn't It?

It's strange, isn't it? It's strange how everything has changed. You probably have read the words of our Savior as found in John 14. But now! Oh, they take on a whole new meaning right now, don't they?

Remember the setting of His words. They took place just a short time before Jesus would go to the cross to die a horrible death for us. Think of what He said.

"Let not your heart be troubled; you believe in God, believe also in Me. In My Father's house are many mansions; if it were not so, I would have told you, I go to prepare a place for you. And if I go and prepare a place for you, I will come again and receive you to Myself; that where I am, there you may be also. And where I go you know, and the way you know" (John 14:1-3).

I've read it many times. I've shared it dozens and dozens of times in the many funeral services I've conducted. But when my Karen died, the words of my Savior took on a whole new meaning.

- There is help and hope for our troubled hearts. It's in getting to know the Lord Jesus Himself in a deeper way (14:1).

- Heaven is real. He called it "My Father's House"! If it wasn't true, He would have told us (14:2a).

- He's preparing a place, a dwelling place, for us where we will be with Him and each other. We will be at home there forever (14:2c-3).

- We know exactly where He is today, and the only way of salvation has been made fully known through His Word (14:4-6).

Knowing WHERE my Karen is, HOW my Karen is today, and WITH WHOM my Karen is brings whole new meaning to the Lord's words in John 14. The same will be true for you as well.

Grab hold of this. When Jesus spoke of Heaven, He called it "My Father's House" (John 14:2). It's the place where the Lord's family is gathering. It won't be long before we'll join them, if you know Christ as your Savior. This profound truth will comfort you as you keep trusting the Lord. Keep eternity in clear view!

Lifeline # 3
You're in a Great Storm. Run to Your Refuge

When I was a teenager, I worked at a camping resort. One particular day I was far from the nearest pavilion as the sky grew very dark. I could hear the sound of thunder as I started my dash! I knew I had waited too long. Suddenly the rain came fast and hard. Hail pounded on my face. The thunder was deafening. The tractor I was driving couldn't go fast enough for me. I could hardly see to drive. By the time I reached the pavilion, I was soaking wet. I wished that I had raced for the pavilion far earlier!

There's something far better than the distant picnic pavilion for us. It is the very present and precious Pavilion of our Lord! He truly wants to be our Refuge.

Think of David who was in a hard spot. He honestly wasn't sure that he was going to get through the terrible situation in which he found himself. As he hid in the cave, the vast army of Saul surrounding him, David viewed the Lord as being his true Refuge.

He ran to his Refuge.

Listen to what he wrote, "I cried out to You, O LORD: I said, 'You are my refuge'" (Psalm 142:5).

Right now it seems like the vast army of sorrow, despair, mourning, and grief not only is surrounding you but drowning you as well under its crushing waves. While it is important to talk about your feelings and tell your story to those who are close to you, keeping busy and staying focused are essential things to get you through the grief process. But there is something even more important than all of these good things.

Run to your Refuge. David cried to the Lord. He called Him "My refuge." This is a powerful picture. This Hebrew word "refuge" is *machaceh* (makh-as-EH) which gives the picture of a shelter, a retreat, a place of safety in the midst of a storm.

There are many things that you and I must do. But the most important thing is to run. Run daily, run often throughout the day to our Refuge, the Lord Jesus Christ.

Grab hold of this. Be honest about your feelings. You are in a storm. Don't just stand there. Run to your Refuge. Cry out to Him just like King David did. "You are my refuge" (Psalm 142:5). Ask for His help. Watch what the Lord is able and willing to do!

Lifeline # 4
Getting Through the Day. Don't Forget This

No two men are exactly alike. While we all share the heartache and sorrow of missing our wives, our experiences vary as well as the particulars of our journey. Some men find the evenings the absolute worst. Others find the days to be long and hard. Still others find both day and night to be unbearable in their sorrow.

Here's something to help you throughout the daytime. One of the Psalmists wrote, "The LORD will command His lovingkindness in the daytime" (Psalm 42:8a).

Commanded lovingkindness may be an expression that is not very familiar to you, but it needs to be! It is a powerful working of the Lord that quietly draws us to Himself.

The word "command" speaks of God's appointment, His action of reaching out to you. How does He reach out to you throughout your day? He does so with *hesed.* That Hebrew word may sound strange, but it is really special. This "lovingkindness", *hesed,* speaks of His love that is loyal for you and that cannot fail.

This doesn't guarantee the absence of our sorrow. It is, however, a very powerful and precious promise that He gives to His people. The Lord Himself promises that His love will be continual, and through this loyal love He will set up appointments to demonstrate His kindness and mercy.

You can become bitter and miss His appointments of the demonstration of His loyal love. Bitterness ruins everything and makes your sorrow even more painful. Go ahead and grieve. Cry hard. Sorrow deeply. But don't miss His loving appointments.

He wants to quiet you with His lovingkindness.

He wants to encourage you with His lovingkindness.

He will work in little details, and sometimes the greatest blessings come unexpectedly.

This is what He loves to do for His children, especially those in difficulty (Psalm 42:6-8a).

Grab hold of this. Cry out to the Lord. Tell Him how much you need Him. Ask Him to enable you to see His loving appointments throughout the day. Sometimes the blessings of His lovingkindness come at unexpected times. Continually He is saying, "I love you forever!"

Lifeline # 5
Can't Sleep? Here's Something for the Middle of the Night

On the previous page we remembered that the Lord commands His lovingkindness in the daytime. This speaks of the ways that the Lord shows His loyal love. For those who aren't resisting the Lord and for those who aren't too busy, the Lord commands these daytime appointments of showing His love for His people.

That's great for the daytime. But what about those in-the-middle-of-the-night moments when you can't sleep?

Many would not even think of it, but we do, don't we? It hurts so very badly as we come to the bedroom and get ready for bed. Once again she's not there any longer. You're lying in the bed where you and your wife shared the joys of the intimate love of marriage. You roll over in the night and reach out to touch her, and she isn't there. Her side of the bed is empty.

What help is there for those in-the-middle-of-the-night experiences when you can't sleep? If you read the first part of the verse on the previous page, it's time to read the last part of the verse right now!

"And in the night, His song shall be with me—a prayer to the God of my life" (Psalm 42:8b).

When you are alone in your bed and can't sleep, talk to your Savior. Even better, sing to Him. I know that some of you are thinking, "I can't sing, and right now, even if I could, I don't want to." Let me gently challenge you to sing to the Lord some of the hymns you've learned. Singing the Lord's songs when your heart is broken is exactly what you need to do.

By faith when you sing to the Lord in the night, you actually are sharing with Him that you are intentionally running to Him, trusting Him, and praising Him because He is worthy. This song of praising Him is exactly what will help you to survive when you think you can't go on. It is the medicine for the wound you are experiencing. It is what every brokenhearted but obedient child of the Lord has done throughout the generations.

"At midnight Paul and Silas were praying and singing hymns to God, and the prisoners were listening to them" (Acts 16:25).

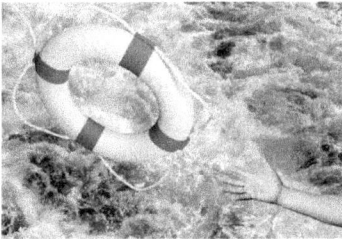

Grab hold of this. Nights are going to be hard. There's no getting around it. But in the middle of the night, in the most difficult time of your life, be a Paul and Silas. Sing to the Lord. Be aware of His worthiness. Don't count sheep. Sing to the Shepherd. It's all right. He will be up all night, even when you eventually fall to sleep.

Lifeline # 6
Promise Me That You Won't Be Bitter Toward the Lord

A few weeks before my Karen went Home to be with the Lord, she was able to sit for a little while on the couch beside me. Obviously, it was a tender time in many ways. She was on constant oxygen. Her breathing was labored and her words became fewer and fewer.

She took my hand and looked at me with those penetrating eyes of hers. Though the cancer had worked in devastating ways, to me she still was the most beautiful lady in all of creation. Her eyes seemed to look straight into my heart just like they always did.

Mustering much of her strength, she whispered, "Michael. I want you to promise something to me. Will you please promise me that when I die, you will continue to love the Lord, serve Him, and not ever allow yourself to become bitter? Promise me?"

Very gently I embraced her and tenderly whispered into her ear, "I do! You've heard me say those words before, haven't you? I do!" She smiled.

On the worst of days for her, she was already projecting what would be the worst of days for me. After being so extremely sick for two years, she knew that soon she would be at her finish line, but I would need to get up and begin to walk on without her. She was concerned about this. She knew that bitterness would make things even harder for me, our children, and our grandchildren.

For over forty-five years we had witnessed people responding to the death of their loved ones. Though there were tears and sorrow, we witnessed some who ran to the Lord, sought His help, trusted Him even when they didn't understand, and were blessed. Sadly, on the other hand, we witnessed people who seemed to resist the Lord, become angry with Him, and become bitter. It was like they were running away from the Lord.

Bitterness is a cancer-like poison that starts with anger and festers into resentment toward a person or a situation. Bitterness can be on a human to human level, and of course, this destroys relationships. Bitterness can also be on a human to the Lord level. "Let all bitterness…be put away from you" (Ephesians 4:31). If you have been bitter, today is the day to give it to Him. Tell Him everything. Give it to the Lord.

Grab hold of this. If you have been bitter toward the Lord, today is the day that you need to get on your knees, man, and confess it to Him. This bitterness will poison you and your relationship with others as well as with Him. "Put it away" on your knees before Him. Ask Him to take the bitterness from you. Think of what Karen whispered, "Promise me that you won't be bitter."

Lifeline # 7
Please, Lord! Either Calm the Storm or Calm Me

Have you ever read in the Bible what is called "The Gospels"? The word "Gospel" means "Good News." Matthew, Mark, Luke, and John are the writers of the four Gospels. Through the wonderful work of the Holy Spirit, these writers were inspired to record the "Good News" of the coming of Christ and His ministry.

While Jerusalem was very special in the life and ministry of the Lord Jesus, much of His public three-year ministry took place around and even on the incredible Sea of Galilee. Also known as the Sea of Kinnereth (Numbers 34:11), the Sea of Tiberias (John 21:1), and the Sea of Gennesaret (Luke 5:1), this very small sea is only eight miles wide at the very largest point and twelve miles long.

Every group that I have taken to Israel has been struck by the beauty of the Sea of Galilee. Sitting almost 700 feet below sea level, this body of water can quickly change from tranquility to a tumultuous storm. Why is that?

The hills surrounding this Sea stretch nearly 1,400 feet above sea level, while the mountains of the Golan Heights, called the Decapolis in the Gospel era, climb more than 2,500 feet. It really is beautiful. However! The winds sweeping over the mountains and through the canyons are capable of producing such sudden and violent storms that even life-long, sea-faring fishermen fear for their lives.

Such was the case one day with the disciples. Picture what happened.

"Now it happened, on a certain day, that He got into a boat with His disciples. And He said to them, 'Let us cross over to the other side of the lake.' And they launched out. But as they sailed he fell asleep. And a windstorm came down on the lake, and they were filling with water, and were in jeopardy. And they came to Him and awoke Him, saying, 'Master, Master, we are perishing' " (Luke 8:22-24a).

What a sight that must have been. The storm was so powerful that the disciples actually used the word for "perishing." The waves were huge. The winds were powerful. The boat was filling with water. Everything was out of control. All hope was lost.

"Even though you are in a storm, don't lose sight of the fact that the Lord Jesus is in the boat with you if you know Him as your Savior."

Maybe today you feel pretty much like this. Indeed, this is a "storm" day for you. It feels like the winds of grief, trouble, and distress are swirling around you to the point that your life is sinking in this sorrow. Now think of this! These terrified fishermen knew Who they needed. He was right there in the boat with them.

Never lose sight of the fact that the Lord Jesus is in this boat with you. You are not alone in the storm. Regardless of how things seem right now, the Lord Jesus is with you in this storm. He's got you. There's no better place to be than with Him in the boat.

"Then He arose and rebuked the wind and raging of the water. And they ceased, and there was a calm" (Luke 8:24b). Their response was one of being stunned, overwhelmed by His authority and convinced of His power. They said to each other, "He commands even the winds and water, and they obey Him" (Luke 8:25).

I've been on the Sea of Galilee when a sudden storm broke out, causing us to make an emergency docking at one of the ports up north. Even though we were never in peril, it was a rough ride back to land.

Our tour bus met us at the docks, and we were glad to hurry on board. When the storm was over, we watched for the next forty-five minutes or so as the Sea of Galilee still was angry with the waves tossing even though the storm was gone.

It was a vivid picture to us of the awesome authority and power of the Lord Jesus Christ. He spoke the word, commanded winds, rebuked the storm and instantly calmed the waves.

This same Lord Jesus cares about you and the storm that you are in. As He calmed the storm on the Sea, He can calm the storm in you as well. Don't run away from Him. Run to Him. Cry out to Him and desire to be close to Him. Watch what He can do in these days in your life.

Grab hold of this. When you are in a storm and your boat seems to be sinking, remember that the Lord Jesus is in the boat with you. Call on Him. He wants to help you. He really does. Picture Him quieting those terrible waves and winds right now. He really is awesome!

Lifeline # 8
Men Who Can Fix Anything and Those Who Can't

Are you one of the guys who can pretty much fix everything and anything? If you are, I want you to know that I hate you! (Only kidding!)

Karen's dad was one of those men. He could work on anything electrical, plumbing, construction or remodeling. Karen's dad could do so many things. He repaired cars with dented fenders, small appliances, leaky roofs, and on and on. All these problems and broken messes could easily be figured out and fixed by her father.

And then she married me! I am one of those men who is not good at fixing any of these problems or working with his hands. You can almost hear me whining, can't you?

I often tell the various repairmen that "men like me keep men like you employed." After making this statement to the furnace repairman one day, he smiled as he looked up at me and said, "Men like me thank men like you for calling us!" We both smiled.

I marvel at the way that the Lord has the ability to fix broken things. Listen to the question He asked Jeremiah. "Then the word of the

LORD came to Jeremiah, saying, Behold, I am the LORD, the God of all flesh. Is there anything too hard for Me?" (Jeremiah 32:26-27).

The question was designed to propel Jeremiah and the people of Judah to run to the Lord, to ask for His help, and to genuinely seek Him even if the circumstances and situations were not what they would have chosen for themselves. Just what you and I need as well.

I don't think I can make it through today. Is anything too hard for the Lord?
I miss my wife more than I ever imagined. Is anything too hard for the Lord?
I am living with regrets that I can't get over. Is anything too hard for the Lord?
I am experiencing emotions I've never felt before. Is anything too hard for the Lord?

You might be one of those guys that seemingly can fix anything, but you cannot fix your broken heart. You cannot handle this by yourself. You need others to walk through this with you, and ultimately, you need the Lord. Just when it looks so overwhelming, He quietly says to you, "I am the LORD…is anything too hard for Me?"

Grab hold of this. The death of your wife is too big, too hard, too deep, too painful, too heart-wrenching for you to fix. Stop trying to handle this. Come to Him and tell Him, "Lord, I really need You. Help me. Please!" He will get you through this.

Lifeline # 9
If God Loves Me So Much, Why Did He Say "No"?

After sustaining serious injuries in a car crash, a well-loved high school student died. Teachers and students alike were devastated. Conversation at the lunch table turned to Luke, known for his love for the Lord. "If God is so loving, why did He not answer our prayers?" one of the students bitterly asked. Conversations quieted, and all eyes were upon young Luke.

"God doesn't always answer prayers the way that we want them to be answered," Luke spoke to the group of teens who now stopped eating to listen. "But He does promise to answer the prayers of His people. For instance, Marsha, when you were a toddler, did your mother say 'yes' to everything you asked?"

Marsha looked up and said, "You've got to be kidding me. Why do you think that my mom told me that the first word I ever uttered to my parents was 'no'? It must be I heard that word a lot."

Luke and his friends smiled at her response. After a moment, he picked the conversation up by reminding his friends, "If you know Christ as your Savior, then you have the absolute promise of God that you can call to Him and He will answer you! It may not be how you have it planned, but it will be the right answer. It might not be the answer that you want, but it will be the right answer."

You might not like these words. After all, you prayed that God would heal your wife. You prayed often that she would get better. And then she died. God said "no" to your earnest pleadings.

The Old Testament prophet, Jeremiah, was in the worst days of his life. Soon Babylon would invade his beloved country. People would die. Others would be taken off into captivity. It was devastating.

However, in the middle of all of this, think of what the Lord said to him. "Call to Me, and I will answer you, and show you great and mighty things, which you do not know" (Jeremiah 33:3). He didn't say to call and I will do whatever you wish; however, He did say that He would answer and unfold His precious plan and purpose in the days ahead. Will you quietly accept the Lord's answer and not resent Him? Asking "why" seems to only make it harder. Ask Him, "'How' am I going to get through this with You, Lord?"

Grab hold of this. Being resentful to the Lord because He said "no" will never be helpful to you or those you love. Will you quietly accept the fact that your Father did indeed hear your prayers? While His answer was not what you wanted, will you by faith trust Him and accept His answer as the right answer?

Lifeline # 10
Oh, Wow! Just What I Need for this Moment

Henry, or Hank, as he was commonly called, sat fidgeting in the counseling center. Appearing to be a wreck, he said to the pastor, "But you don't know what I am facing. I am worried about a lot of things, and I guess I am mad, too," he said without even looking up at the kind pastor.

"I will never say that I know just how you feel," the pastor told him. But in his heart, he had a good idea what the man was experiencing because of the similar struggles through which he himself was also traveling. At the very time of this appointment, both men were traveling a very similar road of disappointment, heartbreak, and sorrow.

The difference between the pastor and Hank was the reaction to their situations. Hank struggled with resentment toward the Lord. He was filled with worry and even began to doubt that the Lord cared about him. Of course he missed his wife. Naturally his sorrow and grief were great. But his emotions were carrying him beyond the typical grief.

Things began to slowly change for Hank when the wise pastor gently asked him, "Hank, do you believe that for the most part King

David was a wise man?" He answered, "Yeah," which is just what the pastor hoped he would say.

Opening his Bible the pastor continued, "Then you will want to know that King David wisely said, 'You are my God…I am Your servant,' according to Psalm 143:10 and 12. When David figured out Who God is and what place the Lord holds, it was easier for him to figure out who he was and what place he should hold."

After a moment the pastor continued, "David didn't live in denial and pretend that he had no problems. He spoke of enemies who were crushing him (143:3), his spirit being overwhelmed (143:4), and plenty of afflictions (143:12). But beginning to view God as being in charge and viewing himself as God's servant then brought David to understanding God's faithfulness and righteousness, according to Psalm 143:1.

It was just what Hank needed: He is God; we are His servants. This is just what you and I need to remember this very moment.

Grab hold of this. There is such release, comfort, and healing when you come to the point of being as wise as David and say, "You are my God, and I am Your servant." Accepting the fact that He is in charge and you are not will begin to quiet your troubled soul. By the way, you'll need to remind yourself of this often! I do as well.

Lifeline # 11
Am I Going Crazy? I've Never Felt So Badly

You are probably experiencing some or all of the emotions of shock, anger, sorrow, pain, loneliness, emptiness (not wanting to go anywhere or do anything), or even times of resentment. You are not going crazy. You are grieving.

You see couples walking together, and some are holding hands, and while you are happy for them, you miss your wife so deeply.

You see couples sitting together in church. Three rows ahead and just to the right, you notice him reaching around and putting his arm around his wife, and oh, how you miss your wife so deeply.

You try eating at your favorite restaurant, and all you seem to see are the couples who are on a date, and how you miss your wife so deeply.

You never knew you could feel this badly, nor did you imagine you could hurt so deeply.

"What level is your thirst for God? The picture of the panting deer is striking!"

There is help. There really is. The help comes, first, as you repeatedly acknowledge your situation and feelings to the Lord and then, second, as you intentionally yearn to grow closer to Him and trust Him in your grief.

The writer of Psalm 42 found himself in a horrible, heartbreaking place. He couldn't stop the tears (42:3). He acknowledged his feelings as he spoke of his soul "being cast down" (42:5). His grief was deep. At this point, he looked to the Lord for help. While it didn't change his situation immediately, nonetheless, it was profound.

In the midst of the worst days of his life, the writer yearned for the Lord and sought Him. He said, "As the deer pants for the water brooks, So pants my soul for You, O God. My soul thirsts for God, for the living God. Why are you cast down, O my soul? And why are you disquieted within me? Hope in God, for I shall yet praise Him for the help of His countenance" (Psalm 42:1,2a, 5).

No, you aren't going crazy. These feelings and emotions are normal. But here's something you must do in your grief. Imagine the deer that is panting for water after being chased. That big old buck is panting deeply for that cold water. Now picture yourself as the buck and the Lord as the cold water.

You might be wondering, "So how do I begin to pant for the Lord? How do I begin to thirst after God? What does that even look like?"

Go back to that big old thirsty buck. He doesn't lie down and lament how thirsty he is. He needs water. Nothing else will satisfy his present and deepest need.

Likewise, nothing else is going to satisfy the deepest need you have. You need the Lord. You need the Lord as much as the panting deer needs cold water. Through anguish of soul, the writer proclaims, "So pants my soul for You, O God. My soul thirsts for God, for the living God" (42:1b-2). What does this mean? How do you begin to thirst for God?

Don't make it complicated.

Bow honestly before Him. Cry out to Him. Ask Him to give you a passion for Him above all else. Ask Him to give you the same desire for Him as a thirsty deer has for water.

Spend time in God's Word. Some have found great comfort and help in listening to the Bible on the audio versions available. He's written you a letter which demonstrates how much He loves you. Listen to Him.

Talk with Him in prayer. Talk with Him often. Only cold water satisfied the thirst of the deer. Only a deepening love and passion for the Lord will help you through these deep emotions. You cannot grow in your desire for Him unless you talk with Him. Tell Him how you are feeling. Ask Him to help you. Thank Him for Who He is and worship Him.

You will always love your wife.

While the dreadful, crushing emotional pain will begin to ease, you will always miss your wife.

But for today, you will get through these significant emotions as you turn to Him. Did you ever imagine that I would tell you to picture yourself as a thirsty buck?

Grab hold of this. Just now, tell the Lord exactly how you are feeling. Pour it all out to Him. Go ahead. But as you are doing this, ask Him to begin to help you have a great desire for Him. Compare it to the thirsty deer. Begin to yearn for Him by asking Him for it. This is the way to walk through grief.

Lifeline # 12
Don't You Wish Someone Would
Tell Your Friends What Not to Say?

Lots of things changed when your wife died, didn't they? Maybe you are discovering that even the way your friends are reacting has changed.

You have read about the profound grief and sorrow of Job. Probably you have also read of his so-called friends who tried to help but who only made matters worse. The Scriptures state, "Now when Job's three friends heard of all this adversity that had come upon him, each one came from his own place" (Job 2:11a). Next, they entered into Job's grief, "They lifted their voices and wept; and each one tore his robe and sprinkled dust on his head toward heaven" (Job 2:12). While none of your friends expressed their grief in this way, probably they have tried to share your sorrow. Notice what they did next. "So they sat down with him on the ground seven days and seven nights, and no one spoke a word to him, for they saw that his grief was very great" (Job 2:13). That was the best thing they could do.

Unfortunately, after seven days they opened their mouths, and everything went downhill from that point. Perhaps so-called friends opened their mouths and said things that were not so helpful to you. Unfortunately, this is pretty commonplace.

Long before Karen became so sick, she was speaking in one of her ladies' retreats. She wrote the following in her notes that she would share with the ladies who attended.

For those who have never ministered to someone going through "deep waters," let me suggest some things NOT to do.
1. Don't say, "I know how you feel" unless you've really been there.
2. Don't ask nosy questions just to satisfy your curiosity.
3. Don't stay for long periods of time unless you really sense God's leading to do so.
4. Don't do all the talking. Learn to listen.
5. Don't give advice unless asked.

I love how Karen had a way of getting to the heart of the matter very quickly. Sometimes it takes me a while to get there. It didn't with Karen! These are good things for us to keep in mind when "bearing one another's burdens." Don't be surprised if someone along the way says something that is unwise, unhelpful, and unsolicited. Commit to never treating others this way.

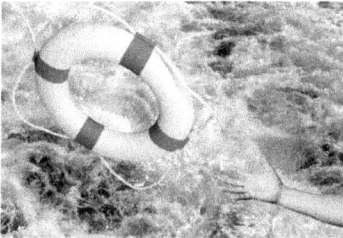

Grab hold of this. If a careless word expressed by a thoughtless person has hurt you, welcome to the club! You can smile as you say to the Lord, "Thank You for understanding me and bearing this burden with me." Take a moment to read Hebrews 4:14, 15.

Lifeline # 13
The Hurt Is Real But So Is the Lord

The terrible news struck him with a blow that crushed him. His business was destroyed and every child of his died the same day. The grief was profound. His name is Job. Think of it.

His horrible trouble. "Then Job arose, tore his robe, and shaved his head; and he fell to the ground" (Job 1:20a). These actions were the way that grief was expressed in the ancient days. All of his oxen, donkeys, and sheep as well as his servants who were tending them were gone in a moment. Then came the crushing news that all of his children were killed in a storm (Job 1:19). He was crushed.

His quiet tenderness. "And fell to the ground and worshipped" (Job 1:20). Stop and let this truth sink in. You are genuinely grieving as one who has experienced the death of his wife. But are you worshipping? What does this even mean?

Job genuinely grieved, but he also worshipped. This word "worshipped" is *shachah* (sha-KHA) which basically means "as the inferior one, I intentionally bow down in love and adoration before my Superior LORD." We do not shake our fists at Him in anger. We do not make rash statements doubting His faithfulness and sovereignty. In our hearts we bow before Him and whisper, "You are God. I am not. You are my God. I bow in reverence to You. Oh, how I need You."

His solid trust. "And he said, Naked I came from my mother's womb, And naked shall I return there. The LORD gave, and the LORD has taken away; Blessed be the name of the LORD" (Job 1:21).

He blessed the name of the LORD. Though the heart-wrenching events were not what he would have chosen, nor did he understand the reason why this was happening, he trusted the Lord. This is so important for you right now today. Job was honest in his feelings of grief, but he was also firm with himself. His feelings were real. His God was also profoundly real to him.

The name of the Lord stands for everything that is revealed to us of God's character, conduct, and purpose. Go ahead and grieve deeply. Just remember Who God is and honestly seek to learn more about Him through the Scriptures.

Grab hold of this. Job's sorrow was real. He grieved profoundly. But Job was also careful to worship. This is a heart action of bowing before Him in trust and love. "In all this Job did not sin nor charge God with wrong" (Job 1:22).

Your author friend is challenged by this. Are you?

Lifeline # 14
Wonderful Help from a Wonderful Person Waiting for You

"Let us therefore come boldly to the throne of grace, that we may obtain mercy and find grace to help in time of need" (Hebrews 4:16).

Over the years my grandfather served his township in several different elected positions. One of those positions was the Justice of the Peace. I actually have the antique roll top desk from which my grandfather heard cases and made judicial decisions.

He was the same person, but he held different positions based on relationship. Let me explain. Before him stood people accused of a particular crime. They knew him as the Judge. Not so for me. After his case was over, I would come into the chambers in his house and stand beside him at his desk. He wasn't my Judge. He was my Grandfather, and we loved each other dearly. What a difference relationship makes.

If you know Christ as your Savior, you will never face Him as the Judge. Rather, He is your loving Lord, and into the Throne Room of His presence you are welcome. We are told not only to come but to come boldly! This is an intentional eagerness, earnestness, and confidence that He really wants you to come!

There you will find mercy, grace, and help in your time of need.

Perhaps you have prided yourself in getting through tough situations before. Perhaps you have boasted of your ability to get through most anything. You've heard others say, "I believed in myself and pulled myself up and got through it." Maybe you haven't actually said these words out loud, but you've thought something pretty close to this.

It won't work this time. Believe me. The death of your wife is too deep, too hard, and too crushing for you to push your way through. You cannot do this on your own. Not this situation. Not this time.

The Lord Himself wants you to come to His throne of grace for help. Come to Him right now. Tell Him just how you are feeling. Tell Him everything. Just let it out and cry. Cry out to Him. You need grace and help. You'll find it at His throne.

Grab hold of this. The help that comes from the Lord doesn't instantly remove the sorrow. However! His help will get you through the worst of times. It really will. Don't try to make it on your own. Come boldly and often to Him.

Lifeline # 15
Give Me Even Just a Little Encouragement Today

Is today an unusually hard day for you?

For me, the days that I thought were going to be extremely difficult weren't as hard as I thought they might be. I'm thinking of days like our anniversary or her birthday or the anniversary of when I asked her to marry me as being days that I was ready with lots of tissues. Surprise! They turned out not to be so bad.

But then, out of the blue, with no rhyme or reason, I am so overwhelmed with how profound the years of Karen's illness were and now the years of her not being with me. On no special occasion, I am a mess. There's no other way to describe it.

Probably you have experienced this, too, haven't you?

Here's a Bible verse and a little note on the word "encourage." You and I both need encouragement. "But command Joshua, and encourage him and strengthen him; for he shall go over before this people, and he shall cause them to inherit the land which you will see" (Deuteronomy 3:28).

Joshua, the future leader of the children of Israel, needed special help. The Lord told Moses to encourage him. It's an interesting word that the Lord used. It's the word *chazaq* (kha-ZAK) which has the idea of being strong, repairing, or being firm. Tender Joshua needed strength and firmness.

That's what encouragement is. When I am disheartened, I am encouraged by intentionally turning to the Lord and depending on Him. When I feel like I am so weak that I can't take another step without my wife, here is what has encouraged me.

"Wait on the LORD; Be of good courage, And He shall strengthen your heart; Wait, I say, on the LORD!" (Psalm 27:14). The idea of "waiting on the LORD" isn't quitting. It isn't becoming lazy and idle. The idea is to intentionally expect, to be awaiting with expectation!

As Joshua needed encouragement to lead the nation, you and I need encouragement to serve the same LORD and look to Him with devotion and expectation. He is God. Settle any question in your mind about this. He really does know what He is doing. He really makes NO mistakes. He really can be trusted.

Grab hold of this. If you want to be encouraged, really wait on Him. Get into His Word. Take time to read Psalm 27, and you will find wonderful encouragements to strengthen and bless you.

Lifeline # 16
Can You Believe That Someone Told Me To
"Keep A Stiff Upper Lip"?

You've probably been told things that just make you shake your head, haven't you? Can you believe someone told tearful, grieving, brokenhearted me, "It's going to be all right. Come on. Keep a stiff upper lip!"

As did I, you might be wondering where in the world that silly expression comes from. According to Dictionary.com, keeping a stiff upper lip means "to show courage in the face of pain or adversity. For example, I know you're upset about losing the game, but keep a stiff upper lip. This expression presumably alludes to the trembling lips that precede bursting into tears."

What a horrible statement for us men who are so crushed and brokenhearted.

Now, let's be clear about something. Others around us have lives. Their lives have gone on and may even be back to somewhat normal since the death of our wives. We can't expect them to be feeling like we are feeling. We certainly do want them to live their lives, don't we?

On the other hand, there is nothing wrong with us crying. In fact, if you haven't cried, I am concerned for you! It's important to cry. Our awesome Creator God has placed within us the release that comes from crying and shedding tears. Even though you know exactly where your wife is, you still miss her more than words can describe. Just when you don't expect it, a memory will come, a thought will enter your mind, a situation will arise and the loss of your wife being with you is so overwhelming that tears just flow. Forget the stiff upper lip. Just cry.

Think of the servants of the Lord and the Apostle Paul who gathered at Miletus. What a precious seaside prayer meeting they had. But notice something extra special.

"And when he had said these things, he knelt down and prayed with them all. Then they all wept freely, and fell on Paul's neck and kissed him, sorrowing most of all for the words which he spoke, that they would see his face no more. And they accompanied him to the ship" (Acts 20:36-38).

They knelt down. That was being intentional in their submissive attitude.

They prayed. That was being intentional in their devotion and trust in the Lord.

They wept freely. That was being intentional in their honesty and transparency.

They sorrowed. That was being intentional as to how they viewed their loss.

Grab hold of this. Forget the stiff upper lip nonsense. Rather, you need to keep a soft, tender heart. Bowing, praying, weeping, and being honest with Him in your sorrow is so important.

Lifeline # 17
I'm Out of Gas and I Can't Go On

When I was a junior in Bible college, I had a tremendous privilege extended to me. I got to preach every Sunday evening in a chapel in downtown Binghamton, New York. My salary was $15 per week and a tank of gas. Originally I was only tasked with preaching. However, as the weeks passed, my love for them grew, and when needs arose during the week, I greatly desired to call on them and minister to them.

As a college student, I didn't have much money. There would be many weeks that my little 1963 Ford ran pretty low on fuel before I was paid.

One such week was really memorable. I had no money, and a significant need arose in one of the families. I prayed about the needle on the dashboard and how it was pointing at E. I still needed to drive to the chapel on Sunday, but this family needed me. So I went. I drove as carefully and gently as possible.

Sunday evening I was paid. No gas stations were open between the chapel and Bible college. As soon as classes were over on Monday, I started the old Ford, and we headed for the gas station. Almost a block away, it started sputtering. Remember, "E" did not stand for "Excellent!" It stood for EMPTY, and empty it was. I was extremely blessed because the gas station was slightly downhill. The sputtering stopped and the motor cut out. I coasted into the station and was glad to stop at the gas pump.

Maybe you are kind of like my '63 Ford. To others that met me on Riverside Drive, everything looked all right. But it wasn't. I was on empty, and honestly, I was in trouble.

We might look like we're doing pretty well to others. After all, we're not crumpled up on the floor weeping and wailing. We are attending church. We go to the grocery store. We smile. We shake hands. We tell people who ask, "I'm doing fine." But really deep down, honestly, we might not be so fine after all. We might be running on empty.

What does that look like?

It isn't always the same for each widower who is starting to run on empty. However, there seem to be several things that are very typical that point to the E on our spiritual dashboards. Do any of these sound familiar?

- Less and less time spent reading or listening to God's Word on audio.

- Fewer and fewer moments talking with Him in prayer.

- Easier and easier to make an excuse why I can't make it to church today.

- More and more time spent in things that have no eternal value and that really aren't even helpful.

- Deeper and deeper feelings of resentment toward the Lord or toward others. "This entire situation is just totally unfair." "Why did my wife have to die?" is becoming a question that is burning into your emotions.

- Procrastinating and putting off those things that really should have been done a week or two ago.

There may be many more things that are taking place in your life that we didn't even begin to address today. Everything might be looking all right to others, but you know if you are running on empty.

I know. I've run on empty.

Here's what continues to help me to "fill up" spiritually in my walk with the Lord Jesus. This isn't a quick fix that you and I must do just occasionally. We often need to fill our spiritual tanks. Here's how from Colossians 3.

"Let the word of Christ dwell in you richly" (3:16a). The idea of "dwelling" is to be right at home with you. Literally, Paul says that we ought not to be strangers with the Word of God. It needs to dwell in us. Because you are in the Word so often, it's like the Word of God is right at home in your life and heart.

My friend, it needs to dwell in you.

My little old '63 Ford was out of gas as I rolled into the station. How full is your spiritual gas tank? The Word of God is the source of our fuel. We need to return to it often throughout the day.

I have found that reading a few extra Psalms has helped me so much. Many of the Psalms are raw with the emotion of what the Psalmist was experiencing but so helpful to see how he trusted the Lord. God's help is ever near, and just as the psalmist needed this, so do we!

Here are just a few of the Psalms that really helped me. I encourage you to take some time to read these. Read slowly and thoughtfully and think about the psalmist's deep trouble and distress. Then see how he turned to the Lord and trusted Him in the situation.

Psalm 3: discovering the Lord's sustaining grace
Psalm 9: getting to know His name and trusting Him
Psalm 18: learning to love Him and see Who He really is
Psalm 23: rejoicing in the fact that He is the awesome Shepherd
Psalm 27: remembering Who He is in our times of waiting

Psalm 37: delighting in the Lord surely is better than fretting
Psalm 40: continuing to say "The Lord be magnified"
Psalm 42: panting after God like a thirsty deer pants for water
Psalm 46: finding quietness because of His very present help
Psalm 61: crying out to Him when the heart is overwhelmed
Psalm 63: seeking the Lord because He is your God
Psalm 73: responding when life isn't fair
Psalm 91: dwelling in the secret place of the Lord
Psalm 100: singing to the Lord even when I don't think I can
Psalm 103: blessing the Lord for Who He is
Psalm 107: lifting our thanksgiving to Him
Psalm 143: meditating on Who He is and what He is doing
Psalm 145: speaking of the wonder of His plan and purpose
Psalm 147: undergoing the healing of our broken hearts
Psalm 150: praising Him because He is worthy

Spend some extra time in the Psalms.

The Gospel of John demonstrates to us the perfect blend of Christ's grace and truth (John 1:14) as He ministered on earth. This is just what we need as well. His Word is true. The Lord Jesus speaks truth to us. Every time you pick up the Bible and read it, you are being surrounded, strengthened, and infused with truth.

But He also is gracious. In His indescribable grace, He extends blessings where they are not deserved. He ministered to those who least deserved it. He gave of Himself to people who were looked down upon, the outcast, the unwanted, the desperately needy. Your Savior is awesome in the balance of His grace and truth. Invest some extra time in the Gospel of John as well as the Psalms.

If you are not into reading, then enjoy listening to God's Word audibly. There is something powerful indeed as we listen to the Word of God being read. This has been such a blessing to me, and I know it will be for you as well.

Grab hold of this. Make sure that the Word of God is "dwelling" in you richly. Don't try living spiritually with the needle pointing toward empty!

Lifeline # 18
Getting Through Today. Embrace the Race

There's a big difference between knowing something and embracing it. One might know that the Lord is sovereign and makes no mistakes. One might know that the Lord does everything right in His own time. One might know that it is important to live for the Lord and know Him in a deeper, closer fellowship. Lots of men know this, but that doesn't necessarily mean that they have embraced it.

Let me explain. To embrace something means "to clasp something in the arms (to embrace a person); to avail oneself (to embrace an opportunity); or to make something one's own by receiving it and believing it (to embrace a spiritual truth)."

It is really powerful to think of the day that the church began. Fifty days after the Lord Jesus rose again, on the Day of Pentecost, the Church age began (Acts 2). Dr. Luke noted, "Then those who gladly received his word were baptized" (2:41). They not only heard the message that Peter preached, they embraced it.

You and I need to gladly receive the Word of God and embrace three things that we need today.

First, embrace the fact that we are appointed to run the race. "Let us run" (Hebrews 12:1a).

Second, "Let us run with endurance the race that is set before us, looking unto Jesus, the author and finisher of our faith, who for the joy that was set before Him endured the cross, despising the shame, and has sat down at the right hand of the throne of God" (Hebrews 12:1b-2).

Third, living the Christian life is a race. The good news is that we are not racing against each other. I'd surely lose! We are in a race with ourselves. Even if we don't want to go on without our wives, we must live for the Lord and finish our race.

I don't want to go on. Life is too hard. It hurts too badly. It just isn't fair. All these thoughts can flood around us to the point that we feel that we are drowning. That's why it says, "Looking unto Jesus." Trust Him. Really turn to Him. Embrace the fact that you are in a race and you MUST keep going with His help. When you most feel like quitting and think that you cannot go on, "look unto Jesus." He has plenty of strength, and His grace is so powerful. You can't do this on your own. That's why you need to embrace the fact that He is in the race with you.

Grab hold of this. "Looking unto Jesus" is not something for others to do. It is what *you* must do each day. Talk with Him about it right now. You'll be glad you did.

Lifeline # 19
You Might Not Look Wooly,
But You Do Have a Good Shepherd

My uncle raised both sheep and cattle on his farm. The difference between the two really struck me as a youngster. Uncle Ed left the cattle unattended in the lower fenced-in pasture. There they'd stay for hours as they grazed and relaxed under the shade trees.

And then there were his sheep! What a different story. Seemingly they couldn't be left alone for more than just a few moments. Those sheep were cute enough to look at, but oh, how they could get into trouble. I am convinced that somehow they had the uncanny ability to find new and surprising ways to get scratched, bruised, and bleeding. They stayed their best when their shepherd was nearby watching over them.

There was something else that struck me as a child. When Uncle Ed wanted the cattle up in the barn, he got behind them and "drove" them with a louder-than-usual voice and a slap or two on their hind quarters. But with the sheep, he simply walked up quietly to the fold, and in a much quieter-than-usual voice he spoke to them as he turned and slowly started walking away.

They immediately recognized his voice and responded to it and followed him up to the barn. There was no driving and no slapping and no raised voice of "HEE!" and "HAA!" He simply talked quietly and walked slowly. He was their shepherd and they followed.

You can already see where this illustration is going, can't you?

Do you remember what the Lord Jesus said? Tenderly He assures us when He said, "I am the good shepherd. The good shepherd gives His life for the sheep. I am the good shepherd; and I know My sheep, and am known by My own" (John 10:11, 14).

It is wonderful to belong to the Lord Jesus. To know that He died, shed His blood, and rose again in triumph over death is such a blessing. His grace is truly amazing. Viewing Him as the Good Shepherd Who gave His life for us helps us to understand how much we mean to Him. The Shepherd loves you, man! He wants to care for you. Picture yourself as a wooly sheep (all right, I know that might not sound helpful, but it is!) and then remember He is *your* Good Shepherd. Tell Him how much you need Him right now.

Grab hold of this! Tell Him that you are glad to be one of His sheep. He wants to help heal your wounds and care for you on your journey. He really does.

Lifeline # 20
He Counts the Stars and Names Them,
But Heals Your Heart, Too

Out of the blue, I just couldn't stop crying. Everywhere I looked screamed to me of Karen's absence from me. Sitting down at my writing desk, I sobbed before the Lord and told Him, "Lord, I am not questioning You, and You already know this, but my heart is broken. I never knew it could hurt so badly."

Later that day I was investing extra time reading in the book of the Psalms. I came upon this: "He heals the brokenhearted and binds up their wounds. He counts the number of the stars; He calls them all by name. Great is our Lord, and mighty in power; His understanding is infinite" (Psalm 147:3-5).

How the Lord spoke to my heart. I didn't stop crying for a very long time, but I was greatly helped. Think of it. Our awesome God spoke the word and the stars were created (Genesis 1:16). He not only created the billions upon billions upon billions of the stars, He has also counted them and named every one of them (Psalm 147:4). That reminded me of how much my awesome LORD knows and how powerful He really is.

But this is what really made me sit back and, through my tears, worship and honor Him. In the midst of His omniscient (all-knowing) view of the stars, He saw my broken heart, and the assurance that He will help me as an individual really spoke to me that day. That reminded me of how much my awesome LORD cares about me as an individual child and how loving and precious He really is.

There are a couple of things to think about as you are reading this. The idea of "brokenhearted" actually means the "smashed, crushed, broken to pieces" heart. The death of our wives is much deeper and more painful than we ever could begin to imagine. It's hard to describe to someone how I am really feeling.

But here's the good news for today. The Lord Jesus really knows how we are feeling, and He wants to and is able to begin to heal our broken hearts. It won't happen overnight. The pain isn't gone by doing three little really quick things. But I can tell you from my experience that the same awesome Lord Who spoke the stars into existence, counted them, and called them all by a different name, cares about you and me. He knows how to slowly, gently, and tenderly heal our broken hearts.

So that promise really blessed me.

But how is He healing my broken heart? Are you ready for this? The answer is that I need to put into practice what I have lovingly told brokenhearted people for the last forty-nine years. I distinctly remember thinking, "Well, Preacher, it is time now for you to preach a little bit to yourself!"

This isn't a magic formula that automatically takes the pain and tears away. However, the Scriptures show us how the Lord uses the medicine of His Word to begin the healing process. Think of this.

When I am overwhelmed, I need to run to Him. He's the Rock. This is my special place.

"When my heart is overwhelmed; Lead me to the rock that is higher than I. For you have been a shelter for me" (Psalm 61:2b-3). When the overwhelming moments flood upon us, we need a higher place on which to stand. We need sure footing and stability. The Lord Jesus truly is the Rock that is higher than we are.

There is a huge void in our lives. A very real part of our lives is now missing from us. We feel incomplete. The emotional pain of sorrow at times is nearly unbearable. This is exactly the time that we refocus.

Focusing on the Lord Jesus and the extent to which He demonstrated His love for us (Romans 5:8) has been such a healing medicine to many of us who are in our situation.

While we will always miss our wives, this refocusing on the Lord Jesus, learning more about Him, growing in our love for Him, and truly believing that as I yield myself to Him He indeed will be my rock are just the right antidote for the pain in our hearts.

When I am sad and downcast, I need to sing to Him. He's the LORD. This is my sincere praise.

"Praise the LORD! For it is good to sing praises to our God; For it is pleasant, and praise is beautiful. The Lord lifts up the humble…Sing to the LORD with thanksgiving" (Psalm 147:1, 6, 7).

It's easy to sing to the Lord and praise Him when everything is going well. It's in the seasons of our lives when our hearts are broken that the song of praise to the Lord is by far the sweetest to Him. Think of all the things for which you can be thankful. Praise Him. Honor and worship Him.

Grab hold of this. To praise the Lord is the start of how He heals the brokenhearted and puts us on solid footing. Are you doing this?

Lifeline # 21
His Grace is Sufficient. It Really is Enough

Sometimes we foolishly think that the Apostle Paul was such a giant of a believer and that, of course, God gave him whatever he asked. Right? Wrong!

We are not sure what it was, but Paul speaks of something that was a "thorn in his flesh and the messenger of Satan." It was really troublesome, whatever it was. Listen to this: "Concerning this thing I pleaded with the Lord three times that it might depart from me. And He said to me, 'My grace is sufficient for you, for My strength is made perfect in weakness'" (2 Corinthians 12:8-9).

God's answer was, "No, My grace will be sufficient."

The word sufficient is *arkeo* which means "to be enough for a thing, to be satisfied or contented with."

You probably feel like there are times when you are on a terrible rollercoaster. There will be moments when you are slowly climbing upward. You're having a better day, and while you are still missing your wife, you really are doing pretty well. You're praising the Lord. You're reading the Bible, and it has blessed you. Something has taken place that has encouraged you. You are climbing upward.

> *"On the worst of days God's grace is powerful and sufficient."*

Then suddenly the jagged-edged reminder pierces you like a sword. She's no longer here with you. You miss the touch of her hand and the sound of her voice. No longer climbing upward, the rollercoaster now plummets with some twists and turns. And you are not enjoying the ride.

Paul pleaded with the Lord to take it away. God said to Paul, "My grace is sufficient." What does that mean and how will it work for us today? Literally, it means that as we look to Him and trust Him, He will help us step-by-step. One day at a time His enabling, powerful grace will be enough for us.

Grab hold of this. He doesn't give you grace today for next week but just what you need right now, this moment. His grace will be enough. He will get you through today as you look to Him. You can rest content in this. It got Paul through the hard times. It will you as well.

Lifeline # 22
What a Profound Difference for Those Who Know Christ

Early in my ministry I was the associate pastor of a large church who had, among many ministries, a weekly television program. A lot of people throughout the Triple Cities area of New York State watched it. As a result, I was asked to conduct many, many funerals of people that I didn't know. Upon meeting them, I discovered that many of them didn't know the Lord.

On a particular week I had several such funerals. Later in the week the senior pastor and I conducted the funeral of one of the dear believers who was a member of the church we pastored. What a difference.

Paul the Apostle explained this to us. He wanted us to understand the blessed facts about our loved ones who trusted Christ to be their Savior. When we understand this, it will be different, oh, so different.

We do not sorrow as others who have no hope (1 Thessalonians 4:13). Our loved ones who trusted Christ are now present with Him. There is coming a glorious day. Paul spoke of it as he wrote, "But I do not want you to be ignorant brethren, concerning those who have fallen asleep, lest you sorrow as others who have no hope. For if we believe that Jesus died and rose again, even so God will bring with Him those who sleep in Jesus. For this we say to you by the word of the Lord, that we who are alive and remain until the coming of the Lord will by no means precede those who are asleep. For the Lord Himself will descend from heaven with a shout, with the voice of an archangel, and with the trumpet of God. And the dead in Christ will rise first. Then we who are alive and remain shall be caught up together with them in the clouds to meet the Lord in the air. And thus we shall always be with the Lord. Therefore comfort one another with these words" (1 Thessalonians 4:13-18).

Don't be confused by the expression of sleep. Our loved ones who trusted Christ are very much awake and rejoicing in Christ's presence. Paul was speaking of the appearance of the body in death when he wrote about being asleep.

We have such assurance and sheer joy as we remember that the day is coming when the event that is called the Rapture of the Church will take place. The body of the dead believer in Christ will rise, and our loved one will be reunited with it. Then quicker than a split second, those who know Jesus will be caught up...listen to this...caught up **TOGETHER WITH THEM** to meet the Lord in the air. I don't know about you, but this old widower can hardly wait!

Grab hold of this. We sorrow. We truly do. But we do not sorrow as those who have no hope. We have great comfort in knowing what is coming. Think about it often today.

Lifeline # 23
He Knows How We Feel. Others Guess. But He Knows

With great enthusiasm, he spoke to me of a delightful invitation and speaking engagement. "Dr. Mike, you won't believe where I recently got to speak! You just wouldn't believe it!" he proclaimed.

"Wow!" I replied. "It sounds pretty exciting."

Before I could say another word, I could tell that he could hardly contain himself as he continued, "I spoke at the First Baptist Church of Marilla, New York. You wouldn't believe it, Dr. Mike. Marilla is not a large town. It's not a big city, and yet there is this beautiful church, a large building full of people that love the Lord."

I'm smiling as I intently listened.

He went on, "They have a beautiful facility, even a large gymnasium. What an outreach they have throughout the area. It is just amazing. Have you ever heard of it, Dr. Mike? You ought to go someday." He concluded as he came up for a breath.

I waited a few seconds before I quietly told him, "For nearly fifteen years I was the senior pastor of the First Baptist Church of Marilla, New York. I am well acquainted with the wonderful church family and facility."

He just stared at me for a few moments. He couldn't believe that I was already acquainted with these dear folks!

In a far greater way, do you know that the Lord Jesus is well acquainted with how you are feeling right now today? You have experienced the death of your dear wife. The emotions of grief ebb and flow, rise and lower, and sometimes the waves of sorrow simply feel like they are going to overwhelm you.

Jesus understands.

Isaiah calls Him "a Man of sorrows and acquainted with grief" (Isaiah 53:3). In fact, He not only is acquainted with grief, "Surely He has borne our griefs and carried our sorrows" (Isaiah 53:4).

Grab hold of this. Today, sit back, close your eyes for a moment, and remember that He is thoroughly acquainted with how you feel. He wants to carry your heavy sorrow, if you will give it to Him.

Lifeline # 24
The 80/20 Principle You and I Are in Right Now

My wife loved to serve the Lord. She enjoyed working one-on-one with ladies in discipleship kinds of ministry. She also enjoyed speaking at various ladies' retreats and seminars.

Karen and I had a great, not perfect, but truly a great marriage. Together, through birth and adoption, we have been blessed with ten children. Additionally, we had the privilege of foster parenting another fifteen children who were not eligible for adoption. As a result of this, Karen was frequently invited to speak to the ladies about marriage, home, family, and how to keep your sanity when things get hectic!

She honestly was dearly loved in the churches we served as well as ladies' retreats and as a conference speaker.

In one of her Bible study journals she wrote out Romans 11:33-34. Let me share this with you. "Oh, the depth of the riches both of the wisdom and knowledge of God! How unsearchable are His judgments and His ways past finding out! For who has known the mind of the LORD? Or who has become His counselor?"

She then entered the following in her study journal.

"In life there seems to be an 80/20 principle. It seems like the situations with which I have little or no control account for the 20% of my life. On the other hand, my response or reaction accounts for the 80% of my life. I must remember His sovereignty (Romans 11:33-34). He is my stronghold (Nahum 1:7). He is my strength (Psalm 27:14)."

You and I had no control over the death of our wives. That is among the 20% situation. Now we are living in the 80% as to how we will respond and react. Sometimes I do better at this than other times. But here is how I want to consistently respond.

"Lord, I trust You. I bow before You. I know that You are in control. You do not need me to tell You what to do! I quietly rest in Your arms. I want to love You more and trust You far greater. Please help me, Lord. Please help me."

Grab hold of this. You couldn't control the 20% events. But you can the 80%. Don't try to do this without Him.

Lifeline # 25
Two Widowers in the Same Pew but Worlds Apart

The Apostle Paul closed his letter to the church family at Rome by stating, "Now the God of peace be with you all. Amen" (Romans 15:33).

It struck him that Sunday morning. The dear pastor glanced up from his hymnal as he was singing praises to the Lord with his church family. The morning service was nearly packed with dear believers who were singing beautifully about the Lord's wonderful peace. Joy flooded his heart as he truly loved these precious folks.

Then he spotted them. There seated side-by-side on the left side of the worship center were the two men that had been widowed in the last year. The widower on the left talked only of his problems. He focused on the uncertainties and difficulties he faced. He seldom read God's Word even though the pastor encouraged him to. He didn't pray. His problems were big, and his focus on the Lord was small.

On the right was another widower. This was a Godly man who lived just the opposite way. His problems actually were more significant, and yet he had a sweet peace about him. He chose to focus on Christ, and he found great comfort in His Word. He was honest in his grief but always giving the Lord praise. Interesting, isn't it?

This is exactly what Paul desired for the Roman believers. He earnestly yearned that they would be acutely aware of the presence and peace of the Lord.

You and I will be like one or the other of those two men.

This doesn't mean that we should clam up and not talk with folks about how we feel. We must. It doesn't mean that we live in denial and pretend that everything is just fine. We must not! It does, however, challenge us to choose the tranquility, serenity, and quietness that the peace of God brings to us.

We sense this more when we are intentionally focusing on Him. He is always with us. We need to be more sensitive to His presence which brings us peace.

Grab hold of this. The God of all glory is with you. As you focus on Who He is and what He wants to do, the more peace you will have from Him.

Lifeline # 26
When the Lord Jesus Brings Us to His Father's House

The Lord Jesus said, "I go to prepare a place for you. And if I go and prepare a place for you, I will come again and receive you to Myself; that where I am, there you may be also" (John 14:2-3).

There is great comfort as well as great joy in His words, isn't there? You probably have found yourself thinking more about Heaven and looking more forward to going there than you ever have before. Many things will take place as we are in the presence of the Lord. Think of just a few of these tremendous blessings.

We will be gazing upon His radiant glory. "Father, I desire that they also whom You gave Me may be with Me where I am, that they may behold My glory which You have given Me; for You loved Me before the foundation of the world" (John 17:24).

"Our future change of address demands a present change of lifestyle! "

We will be gloriously fitted with our new bodies. "For our citizenship is in heaven, from which we also eagerly wait for the Savior, the Lord Jesus Christ, who will transform our lowly body that it may be conformed to His glorious body…" (Philippians 3:20-21).

We will be living in His presence and finally be Home. "And thus we shall always be with the Lord" (1 Thessalonians 4:17). "And they shall see His face" (Revelation 22:4).

You may be thinking, "So, Dr. Mike, that gives me something to look forward to, but how is it going to help me right now? I don't even know how I am going to get through this day. How will this help?" That's an honest question and a good one as well. Here's how it has helped me.

The Apostle John provides the answer when he wrote, "Beloved, now we are the children of God; and it has not yet been revealed what we shall be, but we know that when He is revealed, we shall be like Him, for we shall see Him as He is. And everyone who has this hope in Him purifies himself, just as He is pure" (1 John 3:2-3).

When we begin to understand the tremendous blessing of knowing the Lord Jesus right now, combined with the glories that are awaiting us, it affects how we live and think. This is the intentional pursuit of knowing the Lord and growing closer to Him. It is learning to be pleasing to Him as we trust Him fully. That's John's answer to your question.

Grab hold of this. Our future change of address demands a present change of lifestyle!

Lifeline # 27
Convinced That God Is Just Who He Says He Is

Isaiah was a great Old Testament prophet of the Lord whose ministry spanned decades and no less than four different kings. Warning, pleading, illustrating, and calling to people who spurned his message, few men have ever endured the hardships and heartbreak that Isaiah suffered. And yet Isaiah remained faithful to the Lord.

How did Isaiah do this? The answer is the same for both Isaiah and us today. Isaiah was absolutely convinced that his God is just Who He says He is. Isaiah summed this up when he wrote these words:

"O LORD, You are my God. I will exalt You, I will praise Your name, For You have done wonderful things; Your counsels of old are faithfulness and truth" (Isaiah 25:1-2).

Isaiah was convinced that God is just Who He says He is. That is a wonderful truth and conviction that I hope you likewise have reached in your life. People who know the Lord as their personal Savior and who have settled this matter are folks who are blessed indeed.

In your brokenness, don't forget that you are still blessed. "Not only is He God; He is MY God" was the heartfelt conviction Isaiah declared. He proclaimed both the certainty of his relationship with the Lord as well as the joy that comes from this.

In your grief, don't forget God's grace and His goodness. He has not abandoned you. He is there for you today. He will never leave you. Whisper it often today, "O LORD, You are my God. You are MY very own wonderful, glorious, powerful, loving God."

This won't make today easy.

This doesn't take all the hurt away overnight.

This does make the moment bearable.

Grab hold of this. In the worst of Isaiah's life and times, he found great joy and help in remembering that God is just Who He says He is. You will find the same, and this knowledge will get you through this day. It really will.

Lifeline # 28
Some Say to Follow Your Heart. God Says "Guard It"

I can't believe how often I hear well-meaning people say this. When asked, "What should I do?" by a friend or loved one, frequently the response is, "Follow your heart. Trust yourself."

This is terrible advice!

First of all, you and I know what the Bible says about our hearts. God declares, "The heart is deceitful above all things, and desperately wicked; Who can know it?" (Jeremiah 17:9). In the best of circumstances, our heart is never to be followed because of our wickedness and how easily we are deceived.

Second, right now you and I would say that we are brokenhearted (Psalm 147:3). This would remind us that we need to be careful making big decisions rashly. Sometimes a decision too quickly made is not always the wisest.

So what are we to do? The Bible is very clear. The heart of the matter is that we are to guard it. "Keep your heart with all diligence, for out of it spring the issues of life" (Proverbs 4:23). The idea of the word "keep" is to guard carefully.

We have experienced the death of our wives. Our life has changed dramatically. None of the changes are welcomed by us nor are they enjoyed, are they? We cannot trust our emotions. We cannot follow our hearts. We need to carefully and consistently guard our hearts from many wrong choices.

One of the greatest dangers that we men face is becoming bitter about our situation and hardening our hearts. The writer of Hebrews warns us not to harden our hearts (Hebrews 3:8). This means never allowing ourselves to become obstinate or stubborn. Hardness of heart is a serious condition. It robs us of joy. It wastes our time. It hurts our testimony. It fractures our fellowship with the Lord. It would be a disappointment to our wives.

Guard your heart. Keep it with all diligence. Should you find a growing hardness, go immediately to the Great Physician, read again about His sacrifice for you. Read Ephesians 1 and 2 and ask Him to work in your heart.

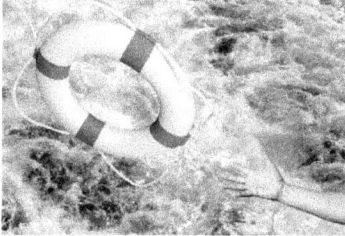

Grab hold of this. You know that a hard heart is NOT going to help. It will only make the hurt greater and more intense. It is a matter of your relationship to the "Son." The "sun" melts butter but hardens the ground. Think about it! I surely am.

Lifeline # 29
Are You Having a *Batach* Kind of Day?

Perhaps one of the most frequently quoted set of verses in the Old Testament would be Proverbs 3:5-6: "Trust in the LORD with all your heart, And lean not on your own understanding; In all your ways acknowledge Him, And He shall direct your paths."

Trusting in the Lord! Men! Do we ever need this in our personal lives and circumstances! Trusting in the Lord is not just a mere nod of our heads toward Him. It's not sitting in church service once in a while and then never giving Him another thought until next Sunday. It is much more than this.

The writer of the book of Proverbs expresses profoundly good counsel to trust in the LORD *wholeheartedly*. Think of it. This word "trust" is *batach* (ba-TAKH) which means "to have confidence in, to feel secure in." I am gripped by this very familiar phrase: "Trust in the Lord with all your heart."

Many years ago, my little girl loved to go swimming as long as she could be in her daddy's arms. She would laugh, splash, and love the water as long as I was holding her. She would squeal, "We're having fun, aren't we, Daddy?"

Do you think I was ever tempted to let her go, drop her, and let her sink? Never! She could *batach*, feel secure in her daddy's arms. The water was far deeper than she was tall. It didn't concern her.

She would not have been able to safely get out of the pool. It never crossed her mind. She was in her daddy's arms, and in the kicking and splashing, she "trusted with all her heart."

Guess what? That is exactly how the Lord wants us to view Him as well. Our situation is too deep for us to handle on our own. Perhaps we've figured a lot of things out and handled many situations throughout our lifetime. Not this time, my friend. Our situation, as much as we hate the word "widower," is just out of our control. We cannot handle this one by ourselves.

But we can trust in the Lord with all our hearts. We can have confidence in and come to grips with the absolute security we have in the Father's arms.

Grab hold of this. If you know Christ as your Savior, picture yourself in the arms of your Heavenly Father. You might not be able to say, "We're having fun, aren't we, Daddy?" However, you will be able to say, "I know that You won't drop me. I am trusting You with my whole heart." Make it, with the Lord's help, a *batach* kind of day.

Lifeline #30
Faith That Pleases the Lord and Gets Me Through Today

The writer of the book of Hebrews stated, "But without faith it is impossible to please Him, for he who comes to God must believe that He is, and that He is a rewarder of those who diligently seek Him" (11:6).

After months of acting the part of the coward, in our senior year of high school I finally got my courage up and asked Karen on a date. I had met her in the third grade, and we had grown up together. She was beautiful and so athletic. I felt clumsy and awkward. I knew that she would say, "No, thank you," and I was fully prepared. I wasn't prepared for her to say, "Yes."

From that first date we never dated anyone else. We sought to include the Lord in our dating as well as got to know each other a little better. I distinctly remember that one night she looked over at me and asked, "So Michael, what is your life verse?"

"Life verse? I've never heard of that!" I responded. "What is your life verse?"

She quietly explained that some folks enjoy picking out a verse that they want to use to describe their life and what they desire the Lord to do. "While I love all the verses, Hebrews 11:6 really speaks to my heart. I'd say that is my life verse," she said.

I had the privilege of being married to this lady for forty-five years. She was not perfect, but she did daily live out the truth of Hebrews 11:6. "Without faith it is impossible to please Him."

Here's how I would define living by faith.

"Faith is knowing my Father and depending fully upon Him. Therefore, I will <u>trust</u> Him even when I cannot see. I will <u>believe</u> Him even when I don't understand. I will <u>obey</u> Him even when the situation doesn't make sense to me."

Stop and think about this, my friend. Faith is knowing and trusting our Father. It results in trusting, believing, and obeying even when nothing makes sense and we don't understand. That's just the point. If we could see, that would be sight. We live by faith.

The more you read God's Word and get to know the Lord, the greater will grow your faith. "So then faith comes by hearing, and hearing by the word of God" (Romans 10:17).

Grab hold of this. "For we walk by faith, not by sight" (2 Corinthians 5:7). We know our Father and depend fully upon Him.

Lifeline # 31
These Tears Aren't Forever

It's different for every man. For me, I didn't think I would ever stop crying. Just when I thought I had cried myself out, they'd start right back up again. It's been over three years since my Karen went Home to be with the Lord. My tears and grieving didn't just begin when she died; they started at her diagnosis and the knowledge that her cancer would not be curable.

You will find that the tears will lessen even though you will always miss your dear wife. Tears are good for us even though they often start up at the most inopportune and unexpected times. Just when you half expect to be teary-eyed, you've been quite surprised that you made it through the situation quite well. Then when you least expect it and for no apparent reason, here they come again.

This is completely normal. You are not going crazy. Honest.

From a human perspective, you and I have experienced the most significant of losses when our wife died. While we haven't really *lost* our wife (we know right where she is!), we have lost the blessing of having her physically with us. This is more profound than any of our friends can imagine, unless it has happened to them.

So we cry. A lot some days!

But these tears aren't forever. There's very good news for us. The Apostle John saw a time coming and described it for us. He said, "And God shall wipe away every tear from their eyes; there shall be no more death, nor sorrow, nor crying. There shall be no more pain, for the former things have passed away" (Revelation 21:4).

No tears allowed. Death exists no more. Sorrow and crying will never be experienced again! All these things are referred to as "former" and that which has "passed away"!

Glory awaits. Does this make today easy? Of course not! However, I want to live as a believer who is blessed by God. While my sorrow and tears are here and now, I want to remember that these are going to be gone someday. We have all of eternity to be with the Lord and our loved ones. With joy we look forward to that day.

Grab hold of this. How awesome is our Lord. He comforts us today. He will wipe away the tears from our eyes some glorious day. I wonder how He will do this. I can't wait. How about you?

Lifeline # 32
You Might Need to Use Your Middle Name on Yourself

Every once in a while I've had to remind myself, "Michael Jeffrey!" (You know that the only purpose of a middle name is for the child to determine how big the trouble he or she is in or how serious the situation is! Hence, I use my middle name!) "Michael Jeffrey, of course you miss your Karen, but you aren't the only one that is experiencing hurt, disappointment, and heartache."

Heartaches come in all sorts of shapes and sizes. Here's a challenge that I try to remember. Behind the many smiles are many different situations of sadness and sorrow. We need to be careful not to let our sorrow blind us to others around us.

A grand day is coming for the believer! Isaiah saw the time coming when the Messiah will rule upon the earth, and in that day His people will experience joy beyond description.

Think of how he described our joy! I love how Isaiah described what sorrow and mourning will do. "So the ransomed of the LORD shall return, And come to Zion with singing, With everlasting joy on their heads. They shall obtain joy and gladness; Sorrow and sighing shall flee away" (Isaiah 51:11).

How awesome is this! They will flee away! Probably we are aware of many right now who are going through very difficult times. Today you may be deeply into sorrow and sighing. This might be the very time that you will need to use your first and middle names as you speak to yourself and say, "Everlasting joy is just ahead. This sorrow and sighing are going to flee away and be gone forever!"

While the glorious truth of this text might not automatically change your situation right now, it will provide the assurance that sorrow is not forever. It will demonstrate that mourning will not be an eternal situation. For me, there is great comfort knowing that pain, sadness, and sorrow are all very temporary. Singing, joy, and gladness will be part of our "forever" with the Lord.

Grab hold of this. The Lord Himself brings joy and assures us that an eternity of joy is ahead for His children. How blessed we are!

Lifeline # 33
Have You Ever Wondered Why Jesus Cried?

"Lazarus is dead" (John 11:14). Such was the solemn announcement that the Lord Jesus made to His disciples. He went on to say, "And I am glad for your sakes that I was not there, that you may believe, Nevertheless, let us go to him" (John 11:15). The Lord Jesus arrived to the news that Lazarus had been dead for four days.

Martha, one of the sisters of Lazarus, rushed to Him and said, "Lord, if You had been here, my brother would not have died" (John 11:21). Not far behind, the other sister, Mary, spoke to Jesus and said, "Lord, if You had been here, my brother would not have died" (John 11:32).

Bless their hearts. They both were actually saying, "Lord, You are four days late."

In your grief, have you ever felt like the Lord was late in coming to you and your situation? It may feel like this. But you and I know, I mean we really do know, that the Lord never makes mistakes. He's never too late.

Let's go back to our text in John 11. The Lord Jesus stood at the tomb of Lazarus in the presence of the beloved sisters and the crowd. A wonderful thing took place. "Jesus wept" (John 11:35).

This is a very brief verse, but it is huge, my friend.

How personal and precious it is to see the Lord Jesus stepping into the hurts and sorrows of those around Him. I am so glad that our Savior is not only 100% the perfect Son of God; He is also 100% man as well. He wept. Was He weeping because He saw the sorrow others were experiencing? I've wondered if it was because He saw, once again, the results of sin coming into His creation. Or do you think it could it possibly be that He wept for Lazarus because He knew that in just seconds He would call Lazarus to come back into this sin-cursed wicked world where Lazarus would once again die someday? Perhaps it was for all three reasons the Lord wept.

Grab hold of this. Your situation is significant to the Lord Jesus. He cares about you and wants to walk with you through this. "Jesus wept." Your sorrow is important to Him. Run to Him. Come often to Him throughout the day. You'll be glad that you did.

Lifeline # 34
Settle Down and Be Still. You'll Discover Something Wonderful

When we are in a full rush, we miss it. When we are simply focused on our troubles, we miss it. When we whine and complain, argue and fuss, we miss it. There is a great blessing, however, when we settle down and learn to be quiet for a few moments. Think of it.

"Be still, and know that I am God; I will be exalted among the nations, I will be exalted in the earth!" (Psalm 46:10).

It is not just for us brokenhearted men. This command, "Be still," is so good for every believer. This word "still" is wonderful, indeed, when we come to realize how powerful it is. The word is *raphah* (ra-FA) which speaks of "relaxing, abating, letting go, hushing and being quiet." When we do this, we know that He is God.

Approximately a year before Karen went Home to be with the Lord, she was having a "good day." She wanted to get out of the house and do something that was "normal." She specifically asked me to take her to our local Christian bookstore. She wanted to be a little independent, so I left her in the gift section and pretended to be looking at books.

I tried not to hover, but she looked up and saw me staring at her. She smiled and waved me on. It was so hard to leave her "alone" a couple of aisles over because she so quickly would sicken. I managed to watch her browse for about ten minutes. During that time I saw her pick up a stone that had our verse today inscribed on it. She insisted that she didn't need it, but I saw her hold it, close her eyes and smile. I went back later and bought it for her. She put it in her pocket on the days of chemotherapy. Being still and remembering Who God is and what He does is very good for us in any situation throughout our day.

Read His Word. Invest some time in the Psalms. Think of what you've read. Be quiet before the Lord. Recall everything you know about Him. Get to know Him better.

Grab hold of this. Friend, I know that you have things that you must do today, but make time to settle down and be quiet. Make it a point to cry out, "Lord, I want to know You better. Help me to hush in Your presence."

Lifeline # 35
These Troubles Aren't Forever

Think of the words that the Holy Spirit moved Paul to pen. "For I consider that the sufferings of this present time are not worthy to be compared with the glory which shall be revealed in us" (Romans 8:18).

The Apostle Paul knew his share of difficulty and hardship. He never lived in denial, pretending that everything was just fine when it really wasn't. Yet Paul had an excellent perception of his difficulties:

- He acknowledged the presence of difficulty. He spoke about "sufferings."
- He carefully considered the situation. "For I consider" which has to do with thinking through the situation.
- He kept eternity in view. Glory awaits the believer. Glory that will be revealed in us is incredible and nearly indescribable.
- He measured the present sufferings as compared to the eternal glory that awaits and remembered that these troubles aren't forever.

It reminds me of the old man who was attending the birthday party of his young grandchild. What an exciting time as the seven-year-old was getting ready to blow out the candles on his birthday cake! The last phrase of "Happy Birthday to you" was just finishing when he looked up and saw his daughter glancing in his direction.

She knew. For years he suffered with a painful condition that worsened as the years wore on. Now even more painful than his chronic physical condition was the pain that he was experiencing because his wife had died several months earlier. It seemed at times that he just couldn't bear another day without her.

He smiled at his daughter because he knew that his pain was not forever, and a wonderful reunion day awaited him. It was nice to know that she cared. It was wonderful to know that these troubles aren't forever. For now, it was back to the party and birthday cake!

Grab hold of this. We do not live in denial of the painful experiences of life. We do, however, seek to keep them in proper perspective of the glory that is coming.

Lifeline # 36
Be Patient. The Train is Coming

Years ago I purchased a vehicle, sight unseen, from a trusted friend who owned and operated a car dealership. At the time Karen and I lived in Elyria, Ohio, and the vehicle we purchased was in Syracuse, New York.

> *"Christ's coming in the air should produce nothing but our eager anticipation. It could be today!"*

I really didn't want to drive that distance to pick up the car and then have Karen drive all the way home by herself. She was a fine driver, but still, that's a long drive in one day. So I had a brilliant idea. Amtrak! I knew that the Amtrak stopped in Elyria within two miles of where we lived. The same train went through Syracuse on the way to New York City.

"The train, Honey. Let's take the train. It will be a special day when we can ride together up to Syracuse and then, of course, we can ride home together. We'll have the entire day without interruptions. In fact, to tell you the truth, Karen, there's something a little romantic about riding the rails through the countryside, holding hands, and enjoying our time together," I told her.

She was sold on the idea.

"By the way, Michael, what time does the train come?" Karen asked a few days before we were to leave. My reply was "2:10." The conversation shifted on to other things.

She didn't ask if it was 2:10 in the morning or afternoon. It was the morning. She really teased and picked on me, pretending to be furious when I told her it was 2:10 in the morning. I assured her that the station platform would be well lit, security would be present, and I wouldn't be surprised if there would be an Elyria police officer or two, and the train would come before we knew it.

None of those things turned out. It was dark. Several lights were out. No security was in view. No train came before we knew it. I wouldn't have felt so uneasy if I were by myself. But my Karen was with me, and we were in a dark and in somewhat of an unsettling place. Where was that train? I kept staring up the tracks looking for that light of the engine. When would it ever come?

It reminds me that "we also eagerly wait for the Savior, the Lord Jesus Christ," according to Philippians 3:20. Face it, friend. We are in a hard place right now. Our circumstances are painful. Our days are long, and nights are even worse. Things that we once enjoyed doing now are just not satisfying. It is like we are standing on a dark Amtrak platform in the middle of the night wondering where in the world that train is.

The train did come. We did hold hands. It wasn't quite as romantic as I had envisioned. But the important point is that the train did come. I looked earnestly for it and was so glad when it happened.

You will not be in this situation forever. When it feels like you are in a dark place and feeling so very uncertain, you need to constantly refocus.

We believe God's Word.

We know Christ as our Savior.

We are convinced that He is coming. We need to be in a state of readiness and watch for Him.

We need to be honest with ourselves. The platform was dark. The middle of the night was frightening. I wanted that train to hurry up and get here. But do you know what? The train arrived when the engineer was ready to pull it into our station. Even so with Christ, we need to be watching and waiting with a good amount of committing ourselves into His care.

Grab hold of this. One of the characteristics of grief is the feeling of emptiness or confusion. Don't deny their existence. Rather, constantly ask the Lord to help you refocus on Him. Be watchful. Today might just be the day that the Lord comes for us.

Lifeline # 37
I Just Feel So Much Regret. Is There Help For Me?

Many men who have experienced the death of their wives experience regret.

- I wish I could tell her one more time how much I love her.
- I wish I would have better communicated to her how much I appreciate her.
- I wish I could have her here to talk with.
- I wish I would have been a better husband.
- I wish I would have been kinder.
- I wish….I wish….I wish…

Feelings of guilt mingled with tremendous feelings of sorrow are apt to sweep up and over us with such intensity that we wonder at times, "Am I really going to survive this?" The tears just won't stop.

The answer really is in God's Word. This won't be easy. It won't be quick. It won't happen overnight. Here's how you are going to get through this if you know Christ as your Savior. You can discover the Lord's help even in the matter of past regrets.

With the Lord's help, you must stop looking back and focusing on the "I wish I had…"

Our Lord used Paul to say this to us. "Not that I have already attained, or am already perfected; but I press on, that I may lay hold of that for which Christ Jesus has also laid hold of me. Brethren, I do not count myself to have apprehended; but one thing I do, forgetting those things which are behind and reaching forward to those things which are ahead, I press toward the goal for the prize of the upward call of God in Christ Jesus" (Philippians 3:12-14).

The idea of "forgetting" gives the picture of not watering the plant and letting it wither. The constant watering of the plant of regret only keeps it alive and flourishing. Constantly re-hashing your perceived shortcomings only keeps the plant of regret alive. We press on and let the past wither by confessing this to the Lord (1 John 1:9) and consistently seeking His help in running the race and looking to the Lord Jesus Himself (Hebrews 12:1-2).

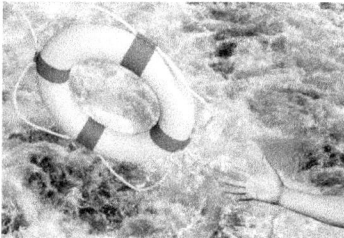

Grab hold of this. You can't run a race by looking backward and wishing for how things might have been. You must look forward. Consistently ask Him for help to "press on."

Lifeline # 38
Won't It Be Grand When Sorrow and Mourning Shall Run Away?

A grand day is coming for the believer! Isaiah saw the time coming when the Messiah will rule upon the earth, and in that day His people will experience joy beyond description. I love how Isaiah described what sorrow and mourning will do.

Think of what he wrote: "So the ransomed of the LORD shall return, and come to Zion with singing; With everlasting joy on their heads: They shall obtain joy and gladness; Sorrow and sighing shall flee away" (Isaiah 51:11).

How amazing. There is coming a grand day when we believers will see our sorrow, crying, and mourning flee away! While the glorious truth of this text might not automatically change your situation right now, it will provide the assurance that sorrow is not forever.

God's Word declares that mourning will not be an eternal situation. For me, there is great comfort knowing that pain, sadness, and sorrow are all very temporary. Singing, joy, and gladness will be part of our "forever" with the Lord.

Think of the phrases of this verse. How wonderful it is to presently be one who is redeemed of the Lord. You are not alone. You belong to Him. He cares deeply for you. If He cared enough for you to come to earth so that He could die on the cross to take the punishment for your sins, don't you think that He is able to help you get through this profound time of sorrow?

Think of the phrases that speak about sorrow being temporary and joy lasting forever. You are walking through the most difficult of situations. Your sorrow is real. Your tears don't seem to want to stop. Often they come at the most inopportune of times! But they aren't forever. Joy can be now as we remember to Whom we belong. It is a special gladness we have because we belong to Him. Joy is also forever.

Grab hold of this. Close your eyes. Picture your present sorrow running away, and thank the Lord for the lasting joy that is ahead. That doesn't automatically change everything right now. But it surely helps. It really does. You'll see.

Lifeline # 39
In Your Sorrow, Don't Lose Sight of What's Precious!

It is important to mourn. The saying that "real men don't cry" is so horrendous. Who in the world ever made up such nonsense? Of course real men cry. It is the really important way that our awesome Creator God built into our systems to express the genuine emotions that we are feeling.

Grieving is important. There may be times that you experience anger, sorrow, a general feeling of emptiness like things just don't matter anymore, loneliness, confusion, or a host of other emotions. This little list is not given in any particular order. You might experience one or two or many on any given day.

It is wise to set aside time each day during these first few months to grieve. Give yourself the opportunity to cry, miss your dear wife, mourn for the hurt you are experiencing, and talk with the Lord about the torn-from-your-life feeling that you are walking through concerning the Homegoing of your wife.

But limit this. Put an actual time limit for which you will aim. Then do something different. Force yourself. Get up and do something. You and I cannot just sit and wallow in our grief. We want to, but the Lord doesn't want us to and neither would our wives.

"When you are grieving, it is easy to lose sight of that which is most important and precious. Be alert, my friend!"

Some time ago I stood before the Council of Baptist Church Planters and spoke to them about "how I am doing now that Karen is Home with the Lord." As of this writing, I am three years into life without having my Karen with me. I still miss her every day. I think of her a dozen times a day, but I've learned that instead of investing energy into being bitter and having an attitude of demanding 'why,' I've really intentionally invested energy into getting to know the Lord Jesus more personally. I want Him to become even more real to me each day. As this takes place, I am becoming more convinced of the blessings that we have in Christ. Here are a few of the many precious things of which we must never lose sight.

- I am blessed far more than I could ever deserve (Proverbs 10:22).

- I am strengthened because I have a Refuge, a Rock that is higher than I and to Him I can flee (Psalm 61:1-2).

- I am comforted knowing that my awesome Lord counts the stars and knows them by name (Psalm 147:4) and comforts the brokenhearted individually (Psalm 147:3).

- I am reminded that my outward man is perishing, but my inward man can be renewed day by day (2 Corinthians 4:16).

- I am quieted by remembering that my affliction is light. It lasts but for a moment. It works for me a far more exceeding and eternal weight of glory (2 Corinthians 4:17).

- I am rejoicing to know that my finish line is closer, and I am challenged to be faithful (2 Timothy 4:7).

- I am confident in my Savior (Proverbs 3:26) and content to be His servant (Psalm 100:2).

- I am accepted in the Beloved (Ephesians 1:6). I am redeemed through His blood (Ephesians 1:7a). I am forgiven (Ephesians 1:7b). I am going to be shown in the ages to come the exceeding riches of His grace in His kindness toward me through Christ Jesus (Ephesians 2:7).

Grab hold of this. We must never allow our grief to blind us from seeing our many blessings. He has "blessed us with every spiritual blessing in the heavenly places in Christ" (Ephesians 1:3). Do not let your pain cause you to miss the precious blessings you have in Him.

Lifeline # 40
Everyone is So Happy and I Feel So Alone and Sad

Many men, even those who have typically been outgoing and the people kind of person, experience a huge difference when the death of their wife comes. Everything looks different. The kind of sorrow that we are experiencing is nothing that we would wish on anyone. We want others to be happy. We want them to enjoy their marriage. We want them to hold hands and hug in public.

Well, kind of. Isn't it surprising the kinds of emotions that arise when we spot a man putting his arm around his wife? To spot a couple laughing together and obviously enjoying their time together sounds so wonderful, and yet it evokes such feelings. Many men are struck with the remorse of opportunities being gone to do this with their wives. Even just seeing a couple sitting together makes us miss our wives so much more.

We foolishly ask ourselves the nagging silent question, "Why is everyone else so happy and everything going so well for everyone else? Why am I the only one that is experiencing this terrible sorrow and loneliness?"

Only those who have experienced the death of their wife could begin to understand how these questions and emotions resonate within us. While they are normal, they also must not be fueled or entertained. Things are not always as they appear. Every couple that you see is not automatically living a carefree life.

Asaph had to have a lesson from the Lord concerning his attitude. You can read his testimony in Psalm 73. He struggled with the question, "Why do the unsaved live so well with seemingly no problems?" On the other hand, why did he have so many problems? It wasn't fair! Then something happened. God brought him back to a proper perspective.

He wrote, "When I thought how to understand this, it was too painful me–Until I went into the sanctuary of God; Then I understood their end" (Psalm 73:16-17). Things are not always as they appear, and the prospect of eternity really changes our perspective, especially people and their situations.

Check out these four things that helped Asaph. God's presence (73:23), guidance (73:24), friendship (73:25), and power (26-28). These are the things that helped Asaph cope with the situations of those around him as he kept focused on the Lord. They will help us as well.

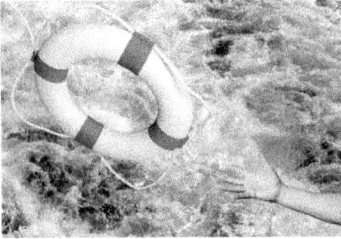

Grab hold of this. When these terrible feelings of jealousy and loneliness strike, immediately go to the Lord. There you will meet the Lord Jesus in the Throne Room. There's lots of help there (Hebrews 4:16).

SECTION SIX

Fifteen Personal Questions
That Widowers Often Have
But Are Afraid or Embarrassed To Ask

Your questions aren't foolish.
It might surprise you to know that
many others are wondering the same thing!

Some questions are easy to answer.
For other questions, there might not be
an answer on this side of eternity.
A wonderful day is coming when we
will meet the Lord.
In that marvelous moment,
all question marks will dramatically become
exclamation points!

Those Fifteen Questions and Answers

#1 Am I the only one that doesn't like to be called a widower?

 # 2 What should I do about my wedding ring? Should I wear it or should I take it off?

 # 3 It breaks my heart to see her clothes hanging in our closet. How did you cope with this and what did you do with Karen's clothes?

 # 4 What are the important things I need to address in our paperwork?

 # 5 How do I handle going to bed without my wife being there?

 # 6 Am I the only one that struggles at church? I feel so profoundly alone.

 # 7 How do I really pursue knowing Christ in a deeper way?

 # 8 Does the Bible really teach that believers who have died are with the Lord right now?

 # 9 What are some decisions that I should make very slowly and deliberately?

 # 10 I don't think I could ever get married again. Is this all right?

 # 11 At first, I thought it was just my imagination, but some of the widows are acting a little too friendly with me. How do I handle this?

 # 12 Is it wrong for me to have coffee with a lady once in a while? Am I dishonoring my wife by doing this?

 # 13 I just don't seem to be able to get moving in the morning. Now that my wife is not here, I don't seem to be motivated like I once was. Are there others who really don't want to keep moving forward?

 # 14 What should I do if I honestly have feelings about taking my life?

 # 15 I've never wanted the Lord to come so much. Is this normal?

#1 Am I the only one that doesn't like to be called a widower?

No! You certainly are not the only man who feels a stabbing of the knife when he is referred to as being a widower. How that title ever came into existence in the first place is a similar question I had.

According to vocabulary.com, a woman whose husband has died is called a *widow*. Similarly, for us men whose wives have died, the label of *widower* is applied. Both widows and widowers are described as being *widowed*. The feminine form of this word came from the Old English *widewe* which means "to be empty."

I don't like the title *widower*. Probably you don't either. I do very much feel the very real empty place in life that Karen's absence has created.

You will continue to discover that there are many adjustments ahead and situations that you will not prefer. Here is what has helped me. When a well-meaning person refers to me as a *widower*, I purpose in my heart not to make a scene and cause embarrassment. I smile and silently remember what Paul called the Roman believers. He said, "Beloved of God, called to be saints!" (Romans 1:7). I whisper to the Lord, "I know that folks view me as a widower. I much prefer your view that I'm not only positionally a saint but also 'Beloved.'" That title will last forever.

2 What should I do about my wedding ring? Should I wear it or should I take it off?

There's not an absolute answer of yes or no to this question. For many of us, the day comes sooner or later when we know that it is time to tenderly remove our ring and store it in a place where it will be cherished. Our wedding ring is another expression of the life we had and enjoyed with our wife. It is a celebration of the most intimate and amazing relationship we could have on earth.

However, the reality is painful, isn't it? The slipping off of your wedding ring can be a time when you cry, mourn, and feel a flood of emotions. But it can also be a time of expressing thanksgiving to the Lord. You have experienced marriage. You can trust God to see His good Hand in what He is doing. It is a time to express again your trust in Him and call for His help in these difficult days.

There is no timeline of when it is time for you to take off your wedding ring. It is one of those things that will probably be sooner, later, or maybe never.

3 It breaks my heart to see her clothes hanging in our closet. How did you cope with this and what did you do with Karen's clothes?

I had wonderful help from my family during those incredibly difficult days. When it came to Karen's clothes, this was something that I knew I wanted to do myself. It's alright if you don't feel this way. But for many of us, caring for her clothes is the last intimate thing we can do for our wives.

Her private articles of clothing I bagged up and discarded. Going through her side of the dresser and removing her private clothing brought a huge flood of tears. I didn't think I was going to survive this. But with the Lord's help I did, and you will as well.

Then it came time to clear her side of the closet. One of the things that helped me was remembering how I lived with a very practical lady for forty-five years. In her practicality and frugality, I knew that she would not want her clothing to simply hang in a closet. She would want them put to use.

It was very hard when my grandson and I drove out of the mission in downtown Cleveland and left her clothes behind. It was another step of accepting the situation. She has gone Home. She is not coming back, but I will see her again. I have to accept the fact that she has died and no longer needs these things. I have to let go. I will never let go of loving her. I will never let go of my memories of her. But as for her clothes, those are the things which I must let go of.

You will have to decide when to clean out her side of the closet. It is nothing that has to be done immediately. But refusing to consider cleaning out her side is not healthy either. It is important to take this step of acceptance. There's nothing wrong with asking your family or a very close friend of hers to help with this, should you need it.

4 What are the important things I need to address in our paperwork?

It just feels so horribly unfair. You are grieving, and the last thing in the world that you want to contend with is paperwork. Don't let it overwhelm you. Work just a little bit at a time, and don't be afraid or embarrassed to ask a loved one or trusted friend to help. In fact, many have found it helpful to surround themselves with a team of people who can advise him. This team might include an elder law attorney, an accountant, a trusted friend or family member, and perhaps your pastor. Sometimes it is hard to make good decisions during those early days of grief.

While I would caution you to move slowly and prayerfully these first few months, there are, however, some things that must be addressed.

Immediate things requiring your attention:

- You will need multiple copies of your spouse's death certificate. The funeral director with whom you worked can help you with this. He will review with you the approximate number you will need. Some of your financial institutions will require this if you are closing out accounts or transferring the name on the investment accounts you have. If you and your wife own your home, you will need the death certificate to transfer title on your real estate. If your wife had life insurance, you will need the death certificate for this as well. Your funeral director will advise you as to what institutions will allow for a copy of the certificate and which will require the original certificate.

- You will need to contact the life insurance company and notify them. Social Security, Medicare, and health insurance companies will need to be notified as soon as possible.
- If your wife tended to pay the bills and keep the checking account, it will be important to push yourself to collect the incoming bills such as utilities, any credit cards, taxes, or loans. Some of these may be electronic, while others may come in the mail. Right now it is hard to even think. Under these circumstances, it would be easy to miss a due payment and incur a late fee. Better to be overly cautious and write on a calendar when the bill is due and when it has been paid.

As soon as you are able:

- If you used your spouse to make financial and health-care related decisions on your behalf, you will soon need to update these papers. You will need to select a new financial power of attorney, a health-care power of attorney, and a new health-care directive clearly stating your wishes.
- Some have suggested that it is important not to make big life-altering decisions for six months to a year, if possible. Usually it is unwise to sell your home in the first month, give away all of your money, and move in with one of your children. The time may come when these decisions must be made (not giving away all your money) but not immediately. You aren't ready for these decisions in the depths of grief unless it is absolutely necessary.

5 How do I handle going to bed without my wife being there?

This is a wound that more men face than you might be thinking. It is one thing to keep busy throughout the day and even when possible into the evening. And then bedtime starts to approach. Her absence is whispered throughout the day, but it shouts at bedtime. Does that describe the situation for you? And you thought you probably were the only one, right? Wrong!

One of the wonderful blessings of a vibrant marriage is the joy of intimacy. I'm not speaking of sexual activity alone. Although that is wonderful, it is only a part of the blessing. Intimacy is the unique closeness that husbands and wives enjoy. It is the expression of this description of Adam and Eve, "Therefore a man shall leave his father and mother and be joined to his wife, and they shall become one flesh. And they were both naked, the man and his wife, and were not ashamed" (Genesis 2:24-25).

It is that time of day when you and your wife would come to your room and prepare for bed. These were moments and experiences that you shared with no one else. You both were reserved for each other. From the undressing to the lying next to each other to the sharing of conversation as you held hands in the dark to the prayers you both prayed to waking up and finding each other the next morning. This is intimacy.

No wonder you miss it so.

Here is what has worked for some men. Some have found that they just needed to battle through this and ask the Lord for special grace. This was a battle that they determined they had to make, and they discovered that His grace is sufficient (2 Corinthians 12:9).

Others trusted the Lord but just could not bring themselves to return to their bed right away. Some moved to a different bedroom in the house. Others swapped beds in their home. A few decided to sleep in their recliner for a little while.

Believe it or not, here's what worked for me. I actually moved to Karen's side of the bed. Although I cried a lot at night, here's what helped. I stayed up until I was really tired. Getting into her side of the bed and talking with my sweet Lord helped me in ways that are hard to describe. You'd think it would make it harder for me, but not so.

Losing the intimacy you once enjoyed with your spouse who is now in Heaven is one of the hardest adjustments that you will face. You will find that His comfort and strength will be just what you need. In time you will look back and see how the Lord has brought you through this. It is one of the hardest adjustments we widowers (I still hate the title, but that's what I am) will face.

I have found the Lord to be so understanding, so willing to help. King David discovered this long before me! He wrote, "The LORD is my strength and my shield; My heart trusted in Him, and I am helped; Therefore my heart greatly rejoices, And with my song I will praise Him" (Psalm 28:7).

In time, as you grow in your love and dependence on the Lord Jesus, you will find the terrible pain of going to bed without your wife will slowly ease. You will always love and miss her; however, you will find that gradually this is going to get easier.

6 Am I the only one that struggles at church? I feel so profoundly alone.

No, you are not the only one to struggle at church. As a believer I love the local church. I've served the Lord Jesus and His local church for nearly fifty years. But I have found in these days, even though I am the preacher, it surely is hard going to church without my Karen. Wow! In the midst of many people, I feel so all alone without her.

There are reasons why it is a struggle to go to church without your spouse.

First, you know that you have three spiritual enemies, and none of them want you in church! All three want to keep you away from the place they hate.

- Enemy number one: (1 John 2:15-17) The world whispers, "You don't need God, His Word or those people at church."

- Enemy number two: (Romans 7:15-25) The flesh whispers, "It's too hard to go to the place that your wife loved so much. Do something that you will enjoy. It won't matter to miss going to church once in a while. After all, you do deserve to be happy, don't you?"

- Enemy number three: (Ephesians 4: 27) The devil whispers, "Don't go today. You can go next week when it is more convenient. Anyway, are you sure that you want to go to a place to worship God when He said 'no' to your prayers? If God is so loving, why would He take your beloved away from you? I'd stay home today if I were you!"

The local church is the place where the family of the Lord gathers. Not only do you need to be there, others around you need you to be with them. Don't let your spiritual enemies keep you away.

Second, you are probably accustomed to having your wife sit next to you. Perhaps you tended to reach over and hold her hand during prayer. Perhaps you reached out and touched her lovingly during the service. Perhaps you remember having her glance your way and smile at you during a hymn or some other time in the service. No wonder it is hard for you to go when now you feel so all alone. Even if you have a dear friend sit with you, which helps, it never changes the fact that your beloved is not sitting next to you.

Third, it is often hard for a widower to go back to his local church because his wife was probably very active in serving the Lord there. Some widowers look up at the choir and miss seeing her there. Other widowers look at one of the musical instruments, and she is not there. Still other widowers walk past her Sunday school classroom where she taught for years, and she is not there. Her absence screams at times to those widowers returning to their local church and makes them feel so very alone.

Fourth, it is often hard for widowers to go back to church, and many times they feel so alone, because their friends don't know exactly what to say. Sometimes they may have almost avoided you because they didn't want to say the wrong thing. Other times, bless their hearts, you might wish that they had avoided you when they said something profoundly thoughtless and hurtful. It is not uncommon for widowers to have these experiences and think, "You wouldn't have said that if my wife was with me." No wonder at times it is hard to be in church and you feel so all alone.

Last (and there are still other reasons that might be unique to you), there is the crushing aloneness walking to the parking lot. Some couples have enjoyed developing special traditions around the Lord's Day services and what they did together after the service. Some enjoy going out to eat. Others enjoy making special meals to be eaten at home after services. Some have enjoyed going to places special to them. Now somehow, none of this is special anymore.

These are some of the things that you and other widowers just like you face when returning to the local church. But you must not allow these to keep you from consistently pushing yourself and being in church.

There are dozens of reasons to push through the aloneness and be in your local church. Let me share just a few.

- We gather because we really are commanded to be there (Hebrews 10:25).
- We gather to worship the Lord which focuses on His worthiness, not on my loneliness and self (Colossians 1:18).
- We gather out of gratitude for what He has done for us (Ephesians 1:7).
- We gather because we need the instruction of God's Word (Isaiah 55:11).
- We gather because there will be music built upon Scripture that will refresh us and help us throughout the week (Colossians 3:16).
- We gather because we want to please the Lord (Colossians 1:10).

Focus on the Lord and pleasing Him. Know that your wife would be proud of you. Know that this is the right thing to do. Go!

7 How do I really pursue knowing Christ in a deeper way?

Don't let this time of deep grieving push you away from the Lord Jesus. Instead of drifting from the Lord, running from Him, or becoming bitter against Him, determine that you are going to run to

Him, depend upon Him, and get to know Him in a closer and deeper way.

The Apostle Paul proclaimed, "That I may know Him and the power of His resurrection, and the fellowship of His sufferings, being conformed to His death" (Philippians 3:10). Paul certainly knew the Lord as his Savior. That's not what he's writing about here. He's sharing the deepest desire of his heart and expressing it as wanting to know the Lord Jesus better, deeper, more intimately. He wanted to learn more about the Lord's will. He wanted to more deeply enjoy the Lord's work. He wanted to demonstrate more consistently the peace that comes through the Lord's will.

You and I need to do this as well. I know you are hurting. I know that probably you don't have a great deal of emotional energy right now. I know that life is so hard that it might sound too difficult to do right now. But you can get to know the Lord Jesus in a deeper way. He wants you to get to know Him better.

How? Let me say right up front that it's not by quickly following a little list once or twice. It is rather by making these principles a consistent part of your life. Even right now, take tiny steps, and in the days ahead you will discover the joy of taking bigger steps.

First, you will need to have a good spiritual diet. This comes from reading, believing, and applying the Bible to daily living. The Bible is food for your nourishment (1 Peter 2:2). It will produce faith (Romans 10:17). It will make you wise (2 Timothy 3:15). I highly recommend that you read right now from the Psalms and Proverbs as well as the Gospel of John. Invest a little time several times a day. You can't grow if you're not eating spiritually.

Second, you must remove any sinful thing that would block or hinder your fellowship with the Lord. Paul warned the Ephesian believers, "And do not grieve the Holy Spirit of God, by whom you were sealed for the day of redemption" (4:30). John describes this removal as "If we confess our sins, He is faithful and just to forgive us our sins and to cleanse us from all unrighteousness" (1 John 1:9).

Third, you will need to consistently exercise spiritually. Little babies must stretch, move, eventually crawl, walk, and then comes running! Responding to stimulation, their little bodies grow, muscles develop, and finally maturity results. Likewise, God has provided opportunities for you to exercise spiritually in order that you might have the joy of getting to know Him better.

Some of the spiritual exercises would include developing a meaningful prayer life (1 Thessalonians 5:17), expressing daily worship of Him (Philippians 2:4-11), imitating the example of your Savior (1 Peter 2:21), serving Him willingly (Psalm 100:2), overcoming sin and temptation through His strength (Ephesians 6:10-13), and witnessing to others about Him (1 Peter 3:15).

Last, the more you ask Him to help you learn of Him (Matthew 11:28-29), love Him (1 Peter 1: 8) and look for Him (Titus 2:13), the deeper will be your fellowship with Him. You can do this, and you'll be glad that you did.

8 Does the Bible really teach that believers who have died are with the Lord right now?

Yes, indeed it does. Paul taught the Corinthian believers that death is not to be feared. He compared our human bodies to a tent (2 Corinthians 5:1), and with the Lord's help, death is as simple as pulling up the tent spikes and taking it down. Then in the verses to follow he goes on to explain that we believers earnestly desire to be Home with the Lord (5:2-7). Wonderfully he then concludes, "We are confident, yes, well pleased rather to be absent from the body and to be present with the Lord" (5:8).

Life was hard for the Apostle Paul, just as it is for you right now. Paul confidently said, "For I am hard pressed between the two, having a desire to depart and be with Christ which is far better. Nevertheless to remain in the flesh is more needful for you" (Philippians 1:23-24). Knowing that he would be immediately present with the Lord brought him such joy and a deep desire to go! But he was also willing to stay until the Lord was ready for him.

While the body rests until the Rapture, the believer is instantly Home enjoying the incredible and indescribable joys of the Lord.

9 What are some decisions that I should make very slowly and deliberately?

Obviously, some of the decisions that involved funeral services, legalities, and paperwork had to be addressed immediately. There are other decisions, however, that you should carefully consider and move slowly and deliberately before making.

Most grief counselors would typically advise moving slowly when it comes to the following things.

- Selling your home and moving away. There are exceptions to this rule. Sometimes it might not be possible for you to live alone. Under those circumstances, don't become stubborn and unreasonable.

- Throwing away things that have been special to you and your wife. The time might come when you will downsize. However, to immediately discard those special keepsakes when you are deeply grieving probably is not the right time. If it is too painful to see them around the house, box them up and put them in a safe place. But go slowly in discarding them.

- Giving all your money away. It may sound strange, but one of the realities of deep grief often compounds the possibility of poor judgment and bad decisions. While it is important to remain generous in your giving, the Lord Jesus doesn't expect you to give away all your funds.

- Making expensive purchases or permanent financial decisions. While it may be necessary to purchase a vehicle or change some funding in your portfolio, try to move slowly in these areas.

Don't be afraid to ask for counsel. Your pastor will be a great source of help. If he doesn't have the answer, it is probable that he knows who can help you make wise decisions.

10 I don't think I could ever get married again. Is this all right?

Here's my answer to this. If I were you, I would simply pray, asking the Lord to help you to do His will in all wisdom and spiritual understanding (Colossians 1:9). Ask Him to help you walk worthy of the Lord, fully pleasing Him (Colossians 1:10). Ask Him to help you to develop a thankfulness to Him (Colossians 1:12). When this takes place, the Lord perhaps will bring into your life a Godly lady that you will love and cherish. Understand this does NOT mean that you will forget about your previous spouse. It does not mean that you will ever stop loving her. But if He desires to do this, you of course will want to do His will.

It is important to understand that the thought of remarrying might be foreign and even unpleasant. So rather than be in a worrisome mode concerning this, right now it is important that you quietly, consistently seek the Lord. He has a plan for you, and it will be just right.

11 At first, I thought it was just my imagination, but some of the widows are acting a little too friendly with me. How do I handle this?

While it is possible that sometimes widows are simply trying to be encouraging and seeking to provide comfort to you, I'm afraid that this quite possibly is not your imagination. Be on your guard and ask the Lord to help you to respond cautiously.

Paul speaks to the Ephesian believers and strongly reminded them, "See then that you walk circumspectly, not as fools but as wise" (Ephesians 5:15). The idea of "walking circumspectly" gives the directive to proceed with accurateness, to be diligent in how you live.

Be on guard at the gathering of your local church. I have personally known of widowers who sense that they have become the targets of unwanted "overly-friendly" widows. Perhaps you have never experienced this, and if so, you might well be thinking, "You've got to be kidding!" But unfortunately, for many widowers this is all too real. And honestly, while it sounds humorous, it really isn't.

Some have had to take steps to avoid unwanted hugs and even unwanted kisses from widows. If you are feeling uncomfortable, then probably you are not just imagining this. Some widowers have actually solicited some help from family or close friends. For instance, if your children are in the area and hopefully attend the same church as you, alert them to your suspicions and ask them to be with you as much as possible when you are there. If you have a trusted friend or a trusted couple, seek to sit with them, if it gets too uncomfortable. Walk out through the foyer with them.

If all of these things fail and the situation continues, I have one more suggestion. You might just have to employ Ephesians 4:15, "But, speaking the truth in love." When unwanted friendliness makes you uneasy, quietly thank the lady for her prayers and concerns and simply share with her how much you are still deeply in love with your wife who is now with the Lord. A quick "Thank you again and good night" might slow things down a little!

12 Is it wrong for me to have coffee with a lady once in a while? Am I dishonoring my wife by doing this?

This question is the opposite of the previous question. The simple answer is no, there is nothing wrong with having coffee or even going on a lunch or dinner date. Often men ask, "How soon is it all right for me to start dating again?" While there is no hard and fast answer, it is often wise to move slowly in this area. Is it wrong to date? No. As hard as it is to say, you are no longer married. Seeing a lady who loves the Lord, who understands that this is a difficult time for you, and who has a good reputation in no way dishonors your wife.

Just don't be swept away into making a hasty decision about a deeper relationship. Understand that your emotions are still jagged and can easily deceive you. Be sure to be honest with the lady as to how this is new territory for you. Ask the Lord to give you wisdom and caution as you navigate through these new territories.

 # 13 I just don't seem to be able to get moving in the morning. Now that my wife is not here, I don't seem to be motivated like I once was. Are there others who really don't want to keep moving forward?

Yes.

When Karen reached the finish line of her race (2 Timothy 4:7), I didn't want to go on without her. I just wanted to stop right there and wait for the Lord to return. We did so much of life together that Karen's Homegoing left a void, an emptiness that was crushing and made it difficult to even think of living without her. There are still times that I cannot imagine going on without her. I've discovered that many widowers have felt the exact same way. You and I are not alone in confessing this.

While it is important to be honest about feeling this way, we must come to several really important and significant pillars of truth upon which we can build our lives.

First, be sure that you really do know Christ as your Savior (John 1:12; 5:24). Only He can give you eternal life. Only through knowing Him will you have life and energy from the Lord for now and eternity. If you truly are a believer, this is the time to grow in your love for Christ and desire to really, really know Him.

Second, picture the scene of a very thirsty deer panting for water. King David described his love for the Lord this way. He wrote, "As the deer pants for the water brooks, So pants my soul for You, O God. My soul thirsts for God, for the living God" (Psalm 42:1-2).

David's description of the parched deer is hard to get out of our minds, isn't it? Either there was a lack of water and the animal was parched or more likely it had been chased and had run for its life. David's experience in the fields no doubt gave him the opportunity to see the deer that outran its predator now being thirsty to the point that it actually pants. This is how he described his desire for God. It is good for us to ask ourselves if we have come to this point of simply "panting for God"! When you ask the Lord to give you such a desire as this thirsty deer, it will begin to help you face days that you didn't think you would ever face! Have you ever prayed something like this to the Lord, "Lord, help me to develop such a love and desire for you that I will become like the deer panting for water." Have you ever prayed such a prayer?

Third, picture the relationship that the Lord Jesus has with you as seen in another of His illustrations. The Lord Jesus truly is amazing in every way. One of the powerful illustrations that He gives provides the dynamic lesson that the energy for living isn't self-produced. In John 15 He points out to His disciples the lesson of the grapevines. He said, "I am the vine, you are the branches. He who abides in Me, and I in him, bears much fruit; for without Me you can do nothing" (John 15:5).

Early in my ministry, I had the privilege of pastoring the First Baptist Church of Westfield, New York. Located in the heart of grape country in Chautauqua County in the southwest part of New York State, I saw vividly the application of John 15. Several of the dear families of this church had acres and acres of those dark blue/purple concord grapes.

They worked all year long to ensure that the life would flow through the vine to the branches in the most productive and healthy way possible. The branch never was responsible for the life-producing grape. This came from the vine. The branch was connected to the vine and displayed the fruit that the vine produced.

Likewise, your healthy fellowship with the Lord Jesus is crucial for the good days as well as for these incredibly, horribly difficult days. Get the picture in your mind of the field of healthy grapevines. Can't you just see the branches that display the beautiful grapes? See how they are connected to the vine? Have you ever prayed something like this to the Lord, "Lord, You are the vine. I am simply a branch. But I want my connection, my fellowship with You, to be growing stronger and healthier. I want You to live through me and the fruit of the Spirit (Galatians 5:22-23) to be showing in my life." Have you ever prayed such a prayer?

Fourth, picture the role of a dedicated soldier. Paul wrote about this to his son in the faith, Timothy. He said, "You therefore, my son, be strong in the grace that is in Christ Jesus" (2 Timothy 2:1). Paul spent so much time under arrest because he was hated for the gospel's sake and falsely accused by unbelievers. During these many times of arrest and confinement, Paul was in the custody of Roman soldiers. Often he was actually chained to one of these soldiers. This gave him the picture that he wanted to pass on to Timothy.

Soldiers serve their country whether it is convenient or not. They serve whether it is fun or not. They obey the voice of their commander, and to the best of their ability they carry out orders. They keep going when it is hard. That's the picture! Have you ever prayed something like this to the Lord, "Lord, You are the commander, and I am one of Your soldiers. Please help me not to distrust or disobey You." Have you ever prayed such a prayer?

If you really want the Lord to help you begin to move forward with Him (never forgetting your wife nor loving her any less), then begin to pray these prayers, asking Him to help you become the thirsty deer, the well-connected branch, and the faithful soldier.

14 What should I do if I honestly have feelings about taking my life?

Please understand, it is completely normal not to want to go on without your wife. BUT if you have any thoughts of taking your life, please, please call your pastor. Call your pastor and be very honest with him about your thoughts. Go and meet with him as soon as you can get there.

You have a purpose in this life. It doesn't feel like it right now, but you do.

You are wanted by family and friends.

You are loved.

You are needed.

You know your wife would not want these thoughts to linger.

Please call your pastor. If he doesn't answer the phone, call the National Suicide Prevention Lifeline at 1-800-273-TALK (8255).

15 I've never wanted the Lord to come so much. Is this normal?

Yes, it absolutely is.

You will discover that eternal things are going to be much more on your mind now than ever before. It will sound strange, but you will discover that sunrises and sunsets will become much more vivid and meaningful. They will become much more beautiful as you consider the Lord's Hand that painted them. You'll catch yourself wondering what it looks like on the other side of the beautiful skies. You will long for Heaven, and you'll be amazed at just how much you want the Lord to come and meet us in the sky.

Another thing will take place if you don't allow bitterness and resentment to overtake your heart. If you will genuinely cast yourself on the Lord, you'll discover a precious desire to count for Him. Counting for Him will be demonstrated by a deepening appreciation of the tremendous sacrifice He made for you. It will be an ever-greater rejoicing in His glorious resurrection. He is the great overcoming Lord. How exciting is this. As these things are taking place, you will see that counting for the Lord will cause the things of this world to mean less and less. You will be less and less rooted to the things of the world. You will sense a growing homesickness for Heaven. While your concern for others around you will cause you to become more sensitive to them, you will find yourself thinking more and more about the eternal.

Frankly, you'll never be the same.

If there are questions that have not been entertained, please feel free to email me at mpeck@bcpusa.org.

SECTION SEVEN

This is How I am Feeling Right Now!
Where in the Bible can I find that lifeline to help me?

Here is a list of some of the
ways that I have felt at times
along with the specific references
in the Bible that continue to help me.

These feelings were especially
raw in the early months
following Karen's Homegoing.
Maybe you can identify with these right now.

You can believe God's Word.
You can absolutely rely on God's Word.
You can be helped by God's Word.

A Guide for When These Things are Happening

When I am wanting to give up…Psalm 11.
When I am feeling so very defeated…Romans 8:28-39.
When I am so lonely I don't think I can stand it…Hebrews 13:5-6.
When I am thinking that I cannot go on…Psalm 73:23-28.
When I am feeling depressed…Psalm 27.
When I am feeling more afraid than ever…Deuteronomy 31:6-8.
When I am struggling in many ways…2 Corinthians 4:16-18.
When I am crushed by being brokenhearted…Psalm 147:1-5.
When I am finding myself worrying about things…Philippians 4:4-8.
When I am wrestling with feeling troubled…John 14:1-3.
When I am beginning to feel bitterness growing…Job 1.
When I am just simply discouraged…Psalm 31:1-7.
When I feel so uncertain and need assurance…Matthew 6:25-34.
When I need direction in life…Proverbs 3:5-6.
When I am battling and wrestling with doubt…Psalm 145.
When I am lacking peace in my thoughts…John 14:26-27.
When I am feeling very weak…Joshua 1:6-9.
When I am experiencing anger…Ephesians 4:26-30.
When I am growing more and more upset…Romans 15:5, 13, 33.
When I am feeling unloved…Ephesians 2:1-7.
When I am feeling overwhelmed…Psalm 61.
When I am needing the Lord's comfort…Revelation 21:1-4.
When I need to admit my need for help…Ephesians 3:16-21.
When I know that I can't do this on my own…Matthew 11:28-30.
When I am under Satan's attack…Ephesians 6:11-18.
When I am feeling bewildered and confused…Colossians 3:14-17.
When I am needing a good reminder…1 Thessalonians 4:13-18.
When I am once again fretting about things…Psalm 37.
When I need to remember that He loves me…Jeremiah 31:1-3.
When I wonder what I should do…Jeremiah 33:3.
When I need to remember that He is God and I am not…Psalm 95.
When I need His strength more than ever…Psalm 28.

When I need to rest in His care…Psalm 23.
When I need to calm down…Psalm 3.
When I need His power…John 15:1-15.
When I need a special blessing and encouragement…Psalm 100.
When I need something to look forward to…John 17:24
When I need to know that God is near…Isaiah 41:10-13.
When I need a push today…Philippians 3:12-17.
When I am homesick for Heaven…Philippians 3:20-21.
When I need to be refocusing on the Lord…Psalm 46:10-11.
When I am still in tears…Psalm 42.

"All Scripture is given by inspiration of God, and is profitable for doctrine, for reproof, for correction, for instruction in righteousness, that the man of God may be complete, thoroughly equipped for every good work" (2 Timothy 3:16-17).

In your brokenness, trust God's Word.
It will be a light to help you.
It will be a GPS to guide you.
It will be a love letter to capture your heart.
It will be food to nourish your soul.

It will encourage you.
It will correct you.
It will challenge you.
It will bless you in ways that you cannot begin to imagine.

Trust His Word.

SECTION EIGHT

It's Time to Settle the
Biggest Decision You'll Ever Make

Do you really know the Lord Jesus as your Savior?

Are you on your way to Heaven?

Heaven! Are You Going There?

I know you have lots to do and many things on your mind, but please, won't you take these few moments to read through this closing question? Think about what the Bible says.
Most people that I have met in my lifetime would say, "I want to go to Heaven someday." But when I ask them, "How would you get there?" the typical answers would be one of the following:

- I think I have been good enough.

- I am trying to keep the Ten Commandments.

- I have been baptized.

- I have joined the church.

- I go to confession, and my minister told me I am forgiven.

While any of these things may sound good to you, would you care to know something very important? The Bible says, "Not by works of righteousness which we have done, but according to His mercy He saved us" (Titus 3:5). Listen to this! "For by grace you have been saved through faith, and that not of yourselves; it is the gift of God, not of works, lest anyone should boast" (Ephesians 2:8-9).

God wanted to make sure that no one in Heaven would be proud to be there because of some great thing accomplished. So the big question is, "If getting to Heaven is not by my good works, how then do I get there?" What do these verses mean when they speak about God's mercy, God's grace, and God's gift?

Let me explain. Please remember this is not my idea. Let me show you straight from the Bible. There are several things you must know.

1. **You must know that every single person is a sinner, including you.** The Bible says, "For all have sinned and fall short

of the glory of God" (Romans 3:23). Sin offends God Who is absolutely, totally holy, pure, and clean.

2. **You must know that your sin separates you from God.** God told Adam and Eve, "Of every tree of the garden you may freely eat; but of the tree of the knowledge of good and evil you shall not eat, for in the day that you eat of it you shall surely die (Genesis 2:16-17).

As you know, even though they had many other trees from which to eat, the day came when Adam and Eve gave in to this temptation. Eve ate because she was deceived, but Adam ate from this tree in defiance of what God had commanded them.

As soon as they ate from that tree, they died spiritually. They no longer enjoyed hearing the voice of the Lord coming in the cool of the day. "And they heard the sound of the LORD God walking in the garden in the cool of the day, and Adam and his wife hid themselves from the presence of the LORD God among the trees of the garden" (Genesis 3:8). Not only did they die spiritually that day, many years later they died physically (Genesis 5:5).

You may be wondering, "So what does that have to do with me?"

It has everything to do with you! That's how sin came into the world. It explains why your parents never had to teach you to disobey. Though I'm sure you were a beautiful baby, you were born a sinner. King David understood this and wrote, "Behold, I was brought forth in iniquity, And in sin my mother conceived me" (Psalm 51:5). The Bible declares, "Therefore, just as through one man sin entered the world, and death through sin, and thus death spread to all men, because all have sinned" (Romans 5:12).

Death is the payment for sin. Listen carefully. Here is the bad news and the good news. "For the wages of sin is death, but the gift of God is eternal life in Christ Jesus our Lord" (Romans 6:23).

The bad news is that because you were born into the human family, you were already a sinner by birth. Later as you began to grow, you became a sinner by action. Your sin alienates or separates you from God. You are in big trouble!

So what is the good news? The good news is that God has a tremendous gift He wants to give you. In just the few minutes you have been reading this, you have read the phrase, "The gift of God" two times. This was found in Ephesians 2:8-9 and Romans 6:23. Here is the great news about God's awesome gift.

3. **While you could never pay the wages of your sin, the Lord Jesus did!** The Lord Jesus said, "For God so loved the world that He gave His only begotten Son, that whoever believes in Him should not perish but have everlasting life" (John 3:16).

- He shed His blood and died on the cross to take your place. "Knowing that you were not redeemed with corruptible things, like silver or gold, But with the precious blood of Christ, as of a lamb without blemish and without spot," (1 Peter 1:18-19). He could do this because He had no sin of His own.

- He actually took your sin upon Himself as He paid for your sin. "Who Himself bore our sins in His own body on the tree" (1 Peter 2:24).

- He paid the price in full. That's why just before He died, He said, "It is finished" (John 19:30).

- Then the great news is that three days later HE AROSE FROM THE DEAD AND BURST FORTH FROM THE TOMB! Listen to the report of the angel who said to the women, "Do not be afraid, for I know that you seek Jesus who was crucified. He is not here; for He is risen, as He said. Come see the place where the Lord lay. And go quickly and tell His disciples that He is risen from the dead" (Matthew 28:5-7).

- This is called "the gospel" which means "good news"! The Apostle Paul said, "For I delivered to you first of all that which I also received: that Christ died for our sins according to the Scriptures, and that He was buried, and that He rose again the third day according to the Scriptures" (1 Corinthians 15:3-4).

4. **Your responsibility is to receive God's awesome gift.** "But as many as received Him, to them He gave the right to become children of God, to those who believe in His name" (John 1:12).

This simply means that you must come to the place today where you admit that you are a sinner. Understand that your good works and great accomplishments can never atone for your sins which separate you from God.

Talk to the Lord right now! In your own words, by faith, right now admit to God that you know you are a sinner. Admit to Him that you know your sins separate you from Him. Acknowledge to God that you believe Christ died for your sins to pay your penalty and that He rose again the third day. Ask the Lord Jesus to come into your life to be your Savior.

You really must trust the Lord Jesus alone to be your Savior. Listen to what He said, "I am the way, the truth, and the life. No one comes to the Father except through Me" (John 14:6).

The decision is yours. You can reject Christ. If you do ignore His gift, you will then face Him at the Great White Throne. Listen to what the Bible says about this, "Then I saw a great white throne and Him who sat on it, from whose face the earth and the heaven fled away. And there was found no place for them. And I saw the dead, small and great, standing before God, and books were opened. And another book was opened, which is the Book of Life. And the dead were judged according to their works, by the things which were written in the books. And anyone not found written in the Book of Life was cast into the lake of fire" (Revelation 20:11-12, 15). The lake of fire is also called "hell," and it lasts forever.

But if you want to be part of the family of the Lord who will be in Heaven forever, then you must place your faith in Christ and trust Him alone to be your Savior. Ask Him to save you right now by coming into your life.

If you do ask the Lord to be your Savior, you actually become part of His family. What a wonderful blessing to know Him and to realize the joy that He alone can give to you! The greatest blessing and source of comfort in these difficult days will be for you to focus upon a personal relationship with the Lord Jesus.

Being a Christian is not following a religion. Rather, it is found in a personal relationship with the Lord Jesus Himself. Through the

Word of God we learn the great Source of comfort and personal help. He is the Lifeline Who will keep you from drowning in grief.

The Lord Jesus said, "Peace I leave with you, My peace I give unto you; not as the world gives do I give to you. Let not your heart be troubled, neither let it be afraid" (John 14:27). He further said, "These things I have spoken to you, that in Me you may have peace. In the world you will have tribulation; but be of good cheer, I have overcome the world" (John 16:33).

He is the ultimate, gracious, powerful Lifesaver. Think of this. If you know Christ as your personal Savior, He is your Lifeguard Who is able to walk on water to come, rescue, and help you through these days.

If you have prayed to ask Christ to be your Savior, please contact us at Baptist Church Planters. Email us at www.bcp@bcpusa.org or phone to let us know at 440-748-1677. We would be very pleased to help you get started in your new life.